THE HIEROGLYPH DETECTIVE

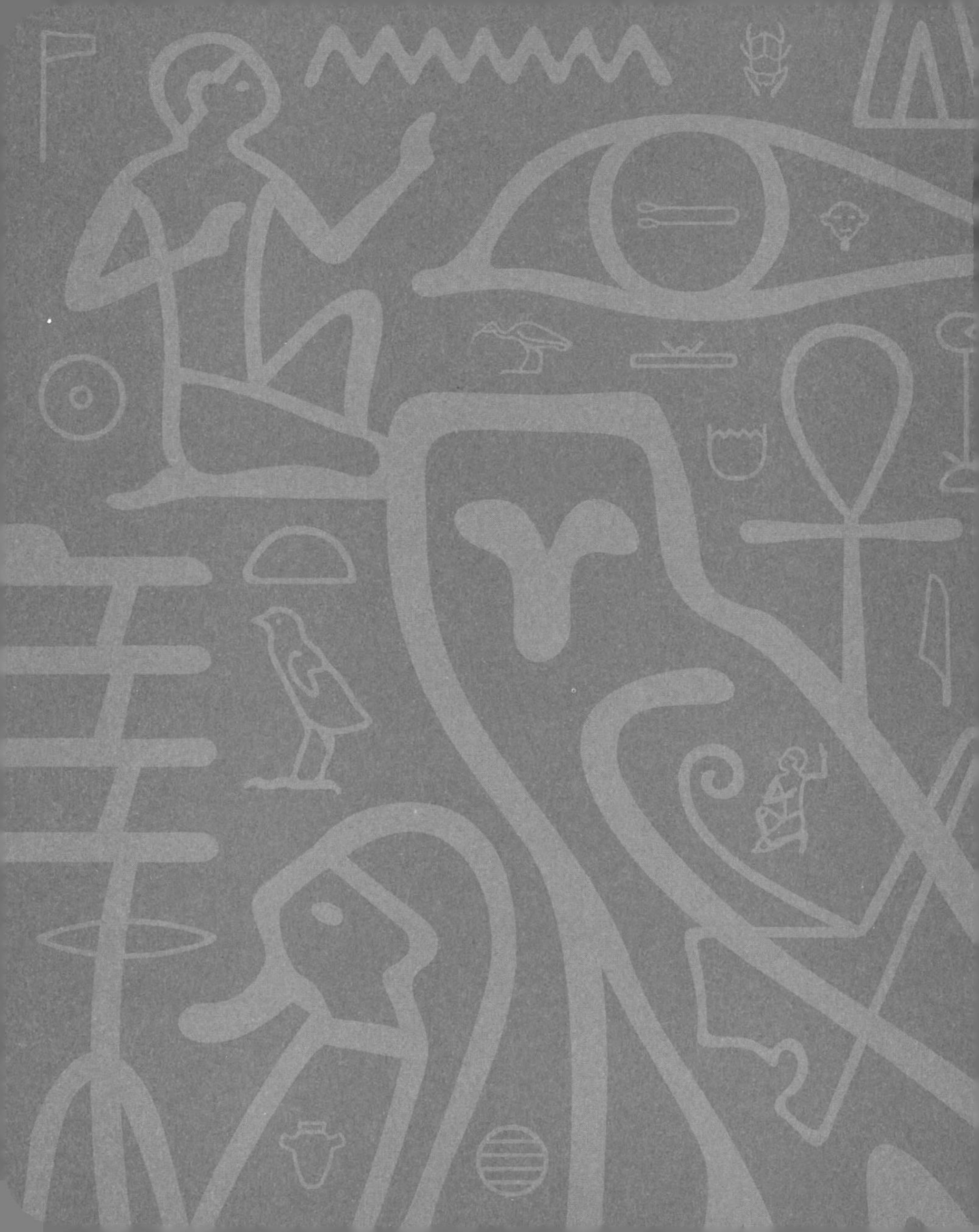

THE HIEROGLYPH DETECTIVE

ADVENTURES IN DECRYPTING THE SACRED LANGUAGE OF THE ANCIENT EGYPTIANS

NIGEL STRUDWICK

DUNCAN BAIRD PUBLISHERS
LONDON

The Hieroglyph Detective
Nigel Strudwick

First published in the United Kingdom and Ireland in 2010 by
Duncan Baird Publishers Ltd
Sixth Floor, Castle House
75–76 Wells Street
London W1T 3QH

Conceived, created and designed by Duncan Baird Publishers

Managing Editor: Christopher Westhorp
Editor: Diana Loxley
Managing Designer: Daniel Sturges
Picture Research: Julia Ruxton

British Library Cataloguing-in-Publication Data:
A CIP record for this book is available from the British Library

ISBN: 978-1-84483-885-1

1 3 5 7 9 10 8 6 4 2

Typeset in Gill Sans and Filosofia
Colour reproduction by Colourscan
Printed in Thailand by Imago

Notes:
Abbreviations used throughout this book: BC Before Christ (the equivalent of BCE Before the Common Era), AD Anno Domini (the equivalent of CE Common Era), b. born, d. died, r. reigned.

The orientation of hieroglyphs in Parts One and Two follow the orientation of the hieroglyphs in the original illustrations in Part Two, but all other hieroglyphs (those that do not appear in illustrations) follow the orientation of the convention established by Sir Alan Gardiner and face left.

CONTENTS

INTRODUCTION

Egyptian hieroglyphs are thought to be the oldest writing system in the world. The earliest examples were found on vessels in a tomb at Abydos in Egypt and date from around 3500 BC. The last dated hieroglyphic inscription is from AD 394 in the temple of Isis at Philae. The script was therefore in use for some four thousand years.

The term "hieroglyph" is derived from the Greek for "sacred writing" and came into use during the period following the conquest of Egypt by Alexander the Great in 332 BC. It differentiated the picture writing from the cursive scripts—from "hieratic," which was used by priests, and "demotic," which was used as the daily, written language (see pages 18 and 19). The images that formed hieroglyphs were derived largely from the everyday world that surrounded the ancient Egyptians—from birds, animals, and the natural world, but also from human-made objects, such as items of royal and divine regalia. The signs were originally written to portray just the things they showed but were later combined to represent words that sounded like the names of the depicted item. Literacy was restricted to a learned elite, which would have included the king and his officials, particularly scribes. It is thought that as little as one percent of the ancient Egyptian population was literate.

OPPOSITE The Rosetta Stone is a granodiorite slab that was unearthed near the town of el-Rashid (Rosetta) in 1799. It is inscribed with the text of a decree in two different languages and three scripts—hieroglyphs (top register), demotic (middle), and Greek (lower). By comparing the Egyptian with the familiar Greek script, scholars were able to gather clues that eventually led to the decipherment of the ancient language by the French academic Jean-François Champollion. His findings were published in 1822.

The historical period in Egypt begins around 3000 BC. It is from this point that the system of dynasties and kingdoms begins, which is one of the main ways of dating Egyptian people and monuments (see timeline, below). At this time, the Nile Valley (Upper Egypt) and the Nile Delta (Lower Egypt) were unified under one controlling authority, the king of Upper and Lower Egypt. (The king's name is uncertain, though he was later mythologized as Menes.)

There do not appear to have been any continuous written texts in this early phase of Egyptian history. However, surviving

KINGDOMS, DYNASTIES, AND LANGUAGE PHASES

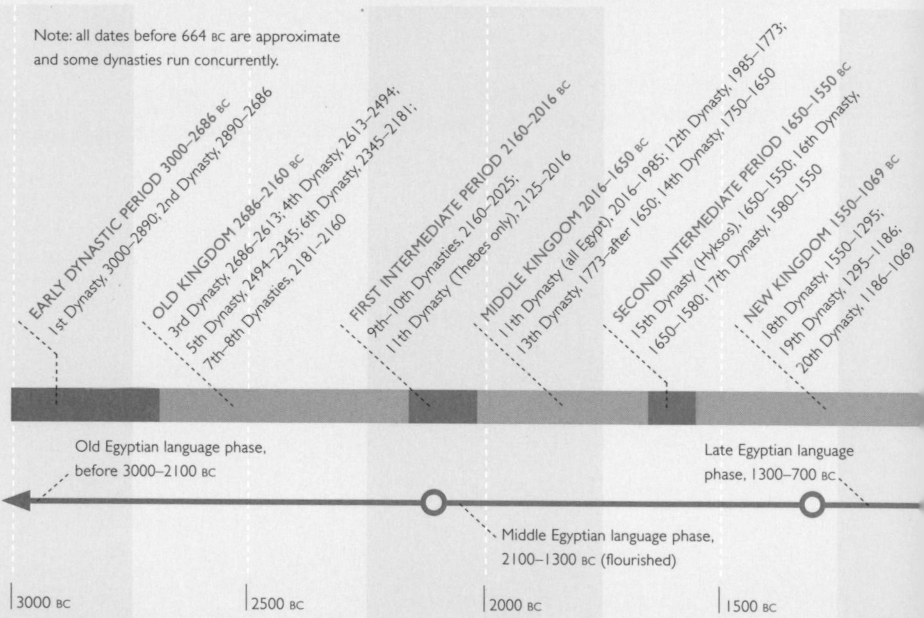

inscriptions on seals and wooden and ivory labels display a combination of isolated hieroglyphs and words. These, together with the images that often accompany them, are decipherable (see the Label of King Den, page 60).

Other early inscriptions consist of names (such as the Peribsen Stela, page 24) and titles. Later texts suggest that records of individual years were being kept as early as the First Dynasty (ca. 3000–2890 BC); the earliest surviving annalistic texts date from the Third Dynasty (after ca. 2686 BC).

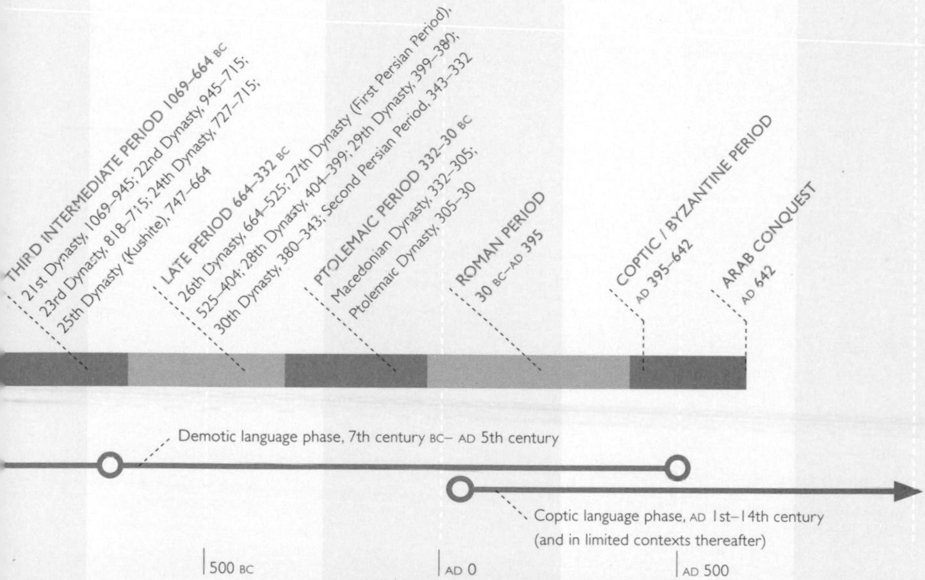

Most knowledge of texts in the next few hundred years comes from tomb inscriptions. In the early Fourth Dynasty (ca. 2600 BC) the first successful attempts were made at composing longer texts, in the form of biographical inscriptions. These offer some insight into the personality and achievements of the tomb owners. The Old Kingdom (ca. 2686–2160 BC) also saw the first administrative texts written in the cursive, hieratic script (see pages 18 to 19), and the first longer religious texts to have survived, known as the Pyramid Texts. These were written in the pyramid tombs of kings to ensure the successful passage of the ruler into the afterlife.

The period of disunity at the end of the Old Kingdom, the First Intermediate Period (ca. 2160–2016 BC), saw the further development of the language, and the composition of longer texts. Among these were the Coffin Texts, religious inscriptions derived initially from the Pyramid Texts, but carved on the coffins of high officials. Following the political reunification of Egypt in about 2016 BC, there were significant developments in the language and changes in grammar and writing. At around this time the first literary texts emerged (these included stories and instruction texts), along with several important archives of administrative and everyday writings.

Texts on papyri, such as letters and other documents from the settlement at Kahun near the Faiyum, from the later Middle Kingdom (ca. 1850 BC), show that the language was continuing to change. By the New Kingdom (ca. 1550 BC), if not before, it is clear that the hieratic that was used to write everyday language continued to develop away from the hieroglyphic forms that were at its root, becoming more cursive all the time—so much so that from about the seventh century BC, Egyptologists have identified a separate script, known as demotic, or "popular" (see pages 19 to 20).

ANCIENT BURIAL RITUALS

Burial rituals played a central role in ancient Egyptian culture and a profusion of hieroglyphic inscriptions appear at sites that are monuments to the dead. Among the most remarkable of burial procedures was embalming, which took place over several weeks. The deceased's major organs (apart from the heart, which was believed to represent intelligence and life force) were removed and the body cavities washed and packed with natron to dehydrate. After forty days the body was washed again, packed with linen and resin, and bound with linen bandages. Oils were an important part of the embalming and burial processes, though exactly which ones were used and in what manner is unclear. But they were included on the ideal list of offerings for the dead (see pages 58 to 59)—typically seven in number, the oils frequently appear at the beginning of the list. Depictions of the same oils would often adorn the tomb walls. From the later Fifth Dynasty on, the names of the oils were also inscribed on small slabs of stone, usually made of alabaster, which were placed in the burial chamber. (The hieroglyph above is a sealed oil jar, which would have served as a determinative [see pages 31 to 33] to mark the end of the name of some oils.)

The first millennium BC saw increasing numbers of Greeks in Egypt, which led to the use of Greek as an important administrative script. This evolved into the final script and language phase of the Egyptian language known as "Coptic," which gradually replaced demotic as the writing of daily life (see page 20). But with the Arab conquest in AD 642, Coptic was itself slowly supplanted by the Arabic language. The last Coptic texts date to around AD 1300.

But what of hieroglyphs in the period ca. 1000 BC–AD 642? Monumental texts continued to be written using hieroglyphs in the Middle Egyptian phase (see page 16) but, particularly in the Ptolemaic and Roman periods (332 BC–AD 395), the range of signs in use increased. The limited number of people able to read hieroglyphs was now shrinking still further, and was probably restricted to temple scribes and priests. With the spread of Christianity, hieroglyphs only continued to appear at sites that were strongholds of the old religious belief (notably the temple of Isis at Philae).

The knowledge of the Egyptian language was lost for many years, although previously unacknowledged discoveries are now believed to have been made by Arab scholars. But with the rediscovery of Egypt by Europe in the eighteenth and nineteenth centuries AD, strenuous attempts were made to decipher the script, helped by the discovery of bilingual inscriptions, such as those on the Rosetta Stone (see pages 6 and 7), which led to major developments in the understanding of the ancient language. The vast numbers of people who now flock to sites throughout Egypt to marvel at the pyramids, temples, and tombs, and the wealth of hieroglyphic inscriptions that adorn them, is testament not only to our continuing fascination with the culture in general but also to the enduring appeal of one of the world's most ancient and intriguing languages.

HOW TO USE THIS BOOK

The aim of this book is to provide a practical, easy-to-follow guide to Egyptian hieroglyphs, giving readers sufficient grounding in the pictorial script to enable them to decipher for themselves some of the many inscriptions they will encounter while pursuing their interest in this fascinating civilization.

The book is divided into three parts. Part One supplies essential background information about the language, including the types of script in use and enough grammar to understand simple texts.

Part Two consists of twenty-three examples of actual texts from the walls of ancient tombs and temples, or on various objects now in major world museums. These texts are presented in ascending order of difficulty, enabling the reader to build up familiarity and confidence with each decipherment. All entries begin with a description of the place or object, providing a cultural and historical context to the selected inscription. This is followed by a step-by-step guide to decoding a numbered, highlighted portion of the text. Each numbered explanatory step begins with three elements in blue: a translation in "CAPITALS," a transliteration in *italics*, and a phonetic (speech sounds) rendering in parentheses. The numbered steps all have corresponding, clearly set out, margin hieroglyphs.

Part Three is a reference section. It contains a thematically organized sign list of most of the hieroglyphs used in the book; a list of hieroglyphs organized by shape; and a short vocabulary.

Note that the orientation of the hieroglyphs in parts One and Two follows that of the accompanying illustrations, where these are present. All other hieroglyphs face left, which is a conventional way to present the signs.

1

1

PART ONE

WORDS OF THE GODS

LANGUAGE PHASES AND TYPES OF SCRIPT

BELOW
Detail from the White Chapel of Senwosret I (see page 80) showing classic hieroglyphs.

Throughout the four thousand or so years in which it was in use, ancient Egyptian was written in various scripts, each of which had a different function. During this time the language itself underwent a series of changes. The different phases of the language are termed Old Egyptian, Middle Egyptian, Late Egyptian, demotic, and Coptic (see timeline, pages 8 to 9). Although these language phases are not of great concern in this book, it is important to know the main types of script used, which are explained in this section.

Hieroglyphs

This book contains other cultural information, but is mostly concerned with hieroglyphs, the Egyptian pictorial script that was used to write the Old Egyptian (ca. 3000–2100 BC) and Middle Egyptian (ca. 2100–1300 BC) language phases. It focuses in particular on Middle Egyptian, considered the "classic" phase of the language. The grammar of this language phase remained fundamentally the same until the last known hieroglyphic inscription of AD 394.

Hieroglyphs were originally used in a wide range of contexts, but it was not long before more easily written scripts were developed. These elaborate and beautiful signs became primarily restricted to monumental buildings—principally palaces, temples, and tombs—but they also occasionally appeared on certain documents. After the knowledge of how to read them had been lost, a number of attempts were made to explain them away as magical symbols representative of esoteric lore. But in this book we will be learning how to see them as building blocks for the writing of a language.

Hieroglyphs are small pictures of people, animals, birds, and objects that were carved with chisels or painted using various brushes, inks, and pigments. The setting out of detailed hieroglyphs involved considerable skill and meticulousness, and a great deal of time on the part of the draftsman, painter, or sculptor. But the ancient Egyptians soon realized that it was easier and quicker to use a brush or a crushed reed pen to produce texts, such as letters and administrative documents, that needed to be written rapidly. The use of these implements inevitably led to a simplification of the script. Egyptologists divide these simplified hieroglyphs from before the first millennium BC into two categories: cursive hieroglyphs and hieratic, both of which are described below.

Cursive hieroglyphs

Cursive hieroglyphs, painted in red or black with a brush, keep the individual signs separate and follow the general design of the original hieroglyphs, but do not have the same level of detail. They are mostly found on papyri of the "Book of the Dead" (a funerary text containing magical spells intended to guide the deceased safely into the afterlife; see pages 18 and 114), and sometimes appear as

RIGHT
A scene from the Book of the Dead of the royal scribe Hunefer (ca. 1285 BC). This is an excellent example of the many magnificent, fully colored illustrations in such papyri showing cursive hieroglyphs from the Middle Egyptian language phase (see page 114).

more elaborate headers on documents that were otherwise written in hieratic. Like the original hieroglyphs, they were used to write the Old and Middle Egyptian language phases.

Hieratic

If one sets out to draw hieroglyphs with a brush, particularly on a small scale, the faster one attempts to write, the more shortcuts one takes with the forms of the signs, and the more likely one is to run signs together. Compare writing a European language in just capital letters or separate lowercase letters with writing continuously in "joined-up" writing. If you think of the liberties many of us take with our writing, imagine how many more one might take

RIGHT
An example of hieratic script from a detail from the Nineteenth-Dynasty Papyrus d'Orbiney.

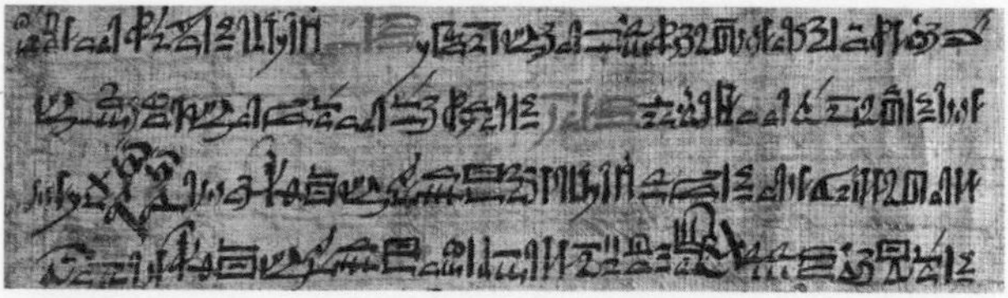

if one were trying to write small pictures! So it is likely that hieratic developed as a result of a simplification of the forms of the original hieroglyphs. These would then have been passed on and gradually adopted. In addition, certain frequently written sign groups acquired their own abbreviated forms. As time went on, hieratic owed less and less to its hieroglyphic originals and developed its own forms. However, it is still usual for Egyptologists to render hieratic into hieroglyphs—a process known as "transcription." Hieratic script was used to write the Old, Middle, and Late Egyptian language phases. Considerable innovations in language were introduced in the Late Egyptian phase (1300–700 BC), which was almost entirely confined to texts written in hieratic script. Many new literary compositions were produced, and an increasing number of everyday letters and administrative texts survive from this time.

Demotic

The writing of hieratic eventually developed so far away from the original hieroglyphic script that Egyptologists cease to call it hieratic. The script known as demotic came into use around the seventh century BC and survived as long as cursive Egyptian was written (which was into the middle of the fifth century AD). "Demotic" is also used for the language phase written in the script of the

LEFT
Demotic script is shown in this detail from a papyrus from the Instruction of Ankhsheshonqy (ca. 100–30 BC).

BELOW
This text is from the Shenute Codex, a seventh-century papyrus written in Sahidic, a Coptic dialect. It tells the story of Shenute (died AD 466), an abbot from the White Monastery at Sohag in Upper Egypt who was influential in the Coptic Church.

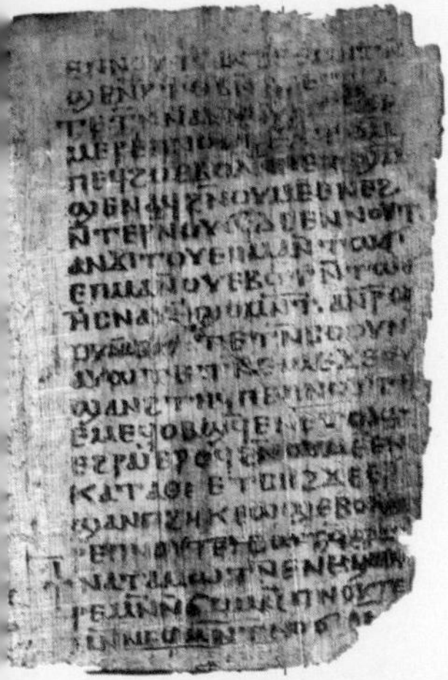

same name, which is in essence a development of the Late Egyptian. Egyptologists tend not to transcribe demotic into hieroglyphs; transliteration is used instead (see pages 25 to 28). Although the older hieratic was still used until the third century AD to write a number of religious texts, demotic became the script of everyday life and was used in a wide range of texts, including commercial, legal, and administrative documents.

Coptic

The Coptic language is a development of demotic and was in use from the first century AD until (in limited contexts) at least the fourteenth century. (It remains in use to this day in certain parts of Coptic church services, and the Coptic community is striving to keep it alive in other contexts.) With the increasing presence of Greeks and the Greek language in Egypt, the attempt was made to write the sounds of demotic using Greek letters. But certain sounds had no Greek equivalents, and special signs were therefore developed to express these; Greek words were also added to represent ideas that did not exist in Egyptian. The resulting script, and the language that it recorded, is called Coptic from the association with the Copts, the adherents of the form of orthodox Christianity that developed in Egypt. However, the earliest recognizably Coptic texts predate the coming of Christianity to Egypt. The scriptures were translated into Coptic, and a number of other religious texts and compositions exist in the language. While Coptic was the language of everyday life, like demotic it was also used for legal, business, and administrative documents.

DIRECTION OF READING AND WRITING

In the modern world we are used to working in languages that can be written in one direction only, usually either from left to right (as in European languages) or from right to left (as in Arabic and Hebrew), although in some contexts it is acceptable to write vertically (in advertising, for example). Speakers of European languages would probably have difficulty reading and writing words from right to left. But ancient Egyptian has far fewer restrictions. Hieroglyphs can be written horizontally or vertically, facing right or left, reading from top to bottom; the only direction that does not normally occur is bottom to top. It is therefore important not to become accustomed to reading in one orientation only.

To find out where to start and which way to read, look at the direction in which the signs are facing—there are usually a few distinctive signs in a text that face in one direction only. The hieroglyphs of humans, birds, and animals are a good place to start. So the two rules to remember are: read from the top to the bottom, and the more distinctive signs point in the direction from which you should start to read.

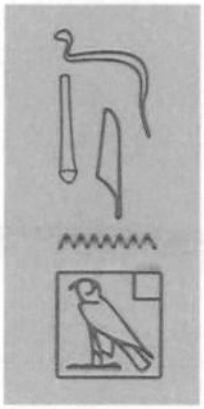

This example is obviously in a vertical column, and reads from top to bottom.  and  very clearly face left, so you should start at the top left, read the higher hieroglyph before the lower one, and move left to right.

The order is thus: 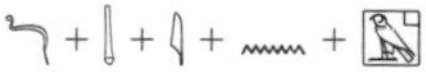

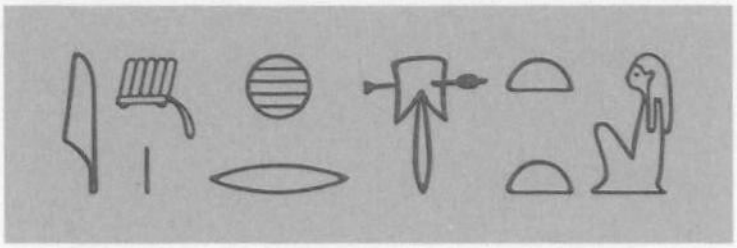

This example is written horizontally, so to find the beginning of the text, look to the end to which  and  point. Then, moving from left to right, read the higher signs before the lower signs. The order is: 

The example on the facing page gives the same text written in four different ways: vertical, facing right and left; and horizontal, also facing right and left. The original version of this text was written in right-facing vertical columns, but for the purposes of this exercise it has been rearranged to demonstrate the other three permutations. The arrangement of the individual signs is therefore different in some places to allow them to follow the different pattern of spaces in the various orientations. Hieroglyphs are a series of pictures, so they can be rearranged slightly without the meaning changing.

Take some time to work out the sequence of signs. With multiple columns, start at the top of the column toward which all the distinctive signs point. With lines, start with the topmost line and begin reading left or right, depending on the orientation of signs.

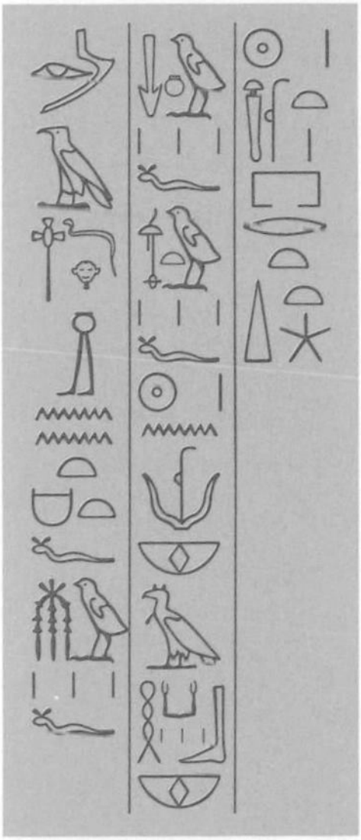

These panels show the same hieroglyphic text arranged in four different orientations. The original version of the text is from a scene in the tomb of Sennefer (Theban Tomb 99, ca. 1420 BC*), one of the "Tombs of the Nobles," on the West Bank at Luxor, Egypt. (See also pages 94 to 97.)*

THE STELA
A stela is an upright stone or wooden slab bearing inscriptions. The *serekh*, or rectangular panel, on this example contains the king's Horus name (see page 38).

THE PERIBSEN STELA

This stela (below) was found in the sand to the south of the tomb of Peribsen at Abydos, and may originally have stood at its entrance. The signs on it, represented above, spell out the name of the king. Two clues are given for the direction in which the signs should be read: the animal on top of the rectangular panel, or *serekh*, should face the start of the text—it faces right. The other clue is the hieroglyph —if you look in the sign list (see page 138), the left–right direction is , so this hieroglyph is also indicating that the text reads from right to left. The orientation is vertical, so read from the top down, and then from right to left.

So the signs are:

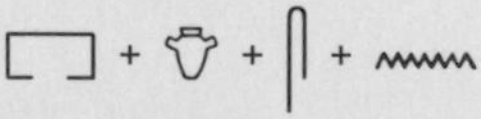

pr-ib-sn

By applying the rule of putting an "e" between the letters of the first and third elements (see page 28), we get the name "Peribsen."

1

PRONUNCIATION AND ORDERING

When confronted with the unfamiliarity of hieroglyphs, it is normal for the beginner to worry about how to pronounce them. One of the challenges that faced nineteenth-century scholars in their attempt to decipher the ancient language was how to establish equivalents between the signs and find a way of representing these signs in Western scripts. Twenty-five discrete sounds were eventually identified, and several of these require diacritical marks above or below the Western letter to express the true sound in one character. (European languages use a variety of accents, or diacritical marks, above and below some letters—such as é, ü, î, ñ, ç—that change the sounds of the letter; even though they are not used in English, they are familiar to many English speakers.) In addition, two extra characters, aleph, ꜣ, and ayin, ꜥ, were introduced for two sounds that cannot be represented in Western scripts. These "sounds" are really just conventional equivalences because we cannot be sure how any of them would have been pronounced.

This system of rendering the letters or sounds of one language into the letters or sounds of another language is referred to as "transliteration." The associated transliteration table (see pages 26 to 27) is arranged according to the sorting order used in modern-day dictionaries of ancient Egyptian, which is based on the different sound groups as defined by linguists. This layout always looks odd to budding hieroglyph readers, used to the A to Z organization of Western European languages, but it is important to learn the order to find words in vocabulary lists. Begin by learning the basic sounds,

TRANSLITERATION TABLE

TRANS-LITERATION	NAMES FOR CHAR-ACTERS NOT PRESENT IN ENGLISH	SINGLE HIEROGLYPH	APPROXIMATE PRONUNCIATION
ꜣ	aleph		a
i͗			i
y		 or 	y
ʿ	ayin		guttural a
w		 or 	u
b			b
p			p
f			f
m		 (less often )	m
n		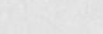 (less often )	n
r			r

h		𓉔	h
ḥ		𓎛	emphatic h (as in "haitch")
ḫ		𓐍	kh (as in "Loch Ness")
ẖ		𓄡	kh (as "ch" in German "-ich")
z		𓊃	z or s (originally z)
s		𓋴	s
š		𓈙	sh
q		𓈎	q
k		𓎡	k
g		𓎼 (rarely 𓎸)	g
t		𓏏	t
ṯ		𓍿	tj (as "ch" in "church")
d		𓂧	d
ḏ		𓆓	dj (as "dg" in "judge")

their order, and the twenty-nine hieroglyphs that indicate them. So the word 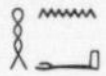 is transliterated as *ḥnʿ*, and  as *ḏd*. In the dictionary *ḥnʿ* will be found earlier than *ḏd*.

These twenty-five sounds do not include the regular vowels (a, e, i, o, u) because vowels were not written in ancient Egyptian. If it is any comfort, some other languages of the Eastern Mediterranean, such as Hebrew and Arabic, are not always written with vowels. But words cannot be pronounced without them, so they must have been included when the language was spoken. It is not known whether the ancient words included the vowels between the consonants, at the beginning, the end, or in a combination of all of them, although scholars have made suggestions based on other languages in which the vowel structure is explicit. However, by sticking with the basic "skeleton" of a word when transliterating it—for example, *nfr*—we do not make too many assumptions about the original pronunciation.

But in order to be able to say these words when talking about ancient Egyptian (in a teaching context, for example), the convention in English is to put an "e," the most common vowel, between most of the phonetic forms of the consonants, which is sufficient to render them comprehensible to the English eye and ear, and to treat *i* as "i," *y* as "y," *w* as "u," and to read the "aleph" and "ayin" as if they were "a." (However, contrary to this rule, the sun god , *rʿ*, is given in this book as Re, which is an accepted alternative spelling to Ra.) So *nfr* is usually pronounced by English-speaking Egyptologists as *nefer*, *ʿnḫ* usually becomes *ankh*, and *ḏd* usually becomes *djed*. Beginners sometimes feel self-conscious when they attempt to pronounce the words for the first time, but pronunciation improves with practice.

SIGN TYPES

Egyptian words are often quite short, although they would have sounded longer with the vowels (see page 28). They are usually composed of a mixture of signs that indicate phonetic value and signs that indicate meaning. In the standard list of some 860 signs, around 300 to 400 have regular phonetic values. But because in origin hieroglyphs are pictures of things they represent, some hieroglyphs can have both a phonetic value and a meaning value. The three main types of phonetic sign are described below.

Uniliteral signs

These are single-consonant hieroglyphs that represent the twenty-five consonantal sounds presented on pages 25 to 28. It is important to memorize uniliterals as they are the most common signs.

Biliteral signs

These two-letter signs are also very common and represent pairs of the twenty-five single consonants. There are several hundred of them, so just a few examples are given in the table below. Along

SIGN	TRANSLITERATION	ROUGH PRONUNCIATION
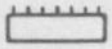	*mn*	men
	*ms*	mes
	*ỉr*	ir
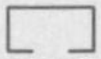	*pr*	per
	*ḥr*	her

with the single consonants, they form the building blocks of a large number of Egyptian words.

The text on pages 34 to 36 explains how to look up a sign's value or usage in the sign lists (pages 124 to 143). After mastering this, you can practice by identifying some of the biliteral signs in the list. Start by looking for the following four signs, and note the readings given there: , , , and . Some of these signs can be found in the texts in Part Two.

To complicate matters, there are a few signs that have more than one reading; thus  can be *ȝb* or *mr*. However, it is possible to work out the correct reading by looking at the signs that accompany it, the phonetic complements and determinatives, whch are explained on pages 31 to 33.

Triliteral signs

These three-letter signs represent groups of three consonants. They do not appear as often as biliterals, but they do include some very common signs, which are shown in the table below.

Use the sign list to find the readings of the following triliteral signs: , , and .

SIGN	TRANSLITERATION	ROUGH PRONUNCIATION
	*ꜥnḫ*	**ankh**
	*nfr*	**nefer**
	*ḫpr*	**kheper**

Combining signs: phonetic complements

Egyptian is not made up just of signs writing one sound. In fact, most words of two or more consonants are not written with the single-consonant signs. More often, a word consists of a biliteral or triliteral sign plus one or more single consonants that "spell out" parts of the biliteral or triliteral sign. The second consonant of a biliteral sign is likely to be spelled out, and the third or the second and third consonants of a triliteral sign are spelled out. For example:

 *pr (per)* and 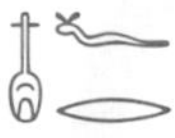 *nfr (nefer)*

As a general rule, when single-consonant hieroglyphs following one of these signs have the same phonetic value as the final sign(s) of the biliteral or triliteral sign(s), they should not be read again. In the previous example, read *pr (per)*, not *prr*, and *nfr (nefer)*, not *nfrfr*. Extra single-consonant signs are known as "phonetic complements" because they complement the sound of the sign they follow.

Phonetic complements show that Egyptian writing is nowhere near as regular or consistent as English. If we added extra consonants to English words, they would become either complete gibberish or another word entirely. Egyptian writing is far more flexible, and scribes could often miss the complements entirely, especially if space was short; however, if they had space to fill, they could use additional signs without affecting the meaning.

Determinatives and whole-word signs

Something that is alien to a totally phonetic language like English is the possibility that a sign has a sense value (a meaning) rather than

The papyrus roll determines abstract words or concepts such as:

ỉp, "to count."

Legs determine many words that have some association with movement. For example:

pr, "to go."

The leg can determine the noun *ḫnd*, "calf of the leg," as well as the verb

ḫnd, "to tread."

The seated man can be the determinative for personal names and of words for "man" and related concepts such as "people" or the occupations of man. It can also be used to determine the whole of a personal name. For example:

ỉmn-ḥtp, "Amenhotep."

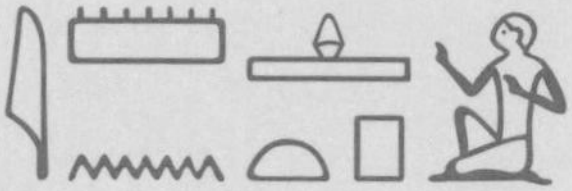

a sound value. But in ancient Egyptian, sense-value/meaning signs, or determinatives, are sometimes written at the end of a word, and their pictorial nature helps the reader determine more clearly the meaning of the word that has gone before. Sometimes the determinative is a direct depiction of the meaning of the word (for example, in 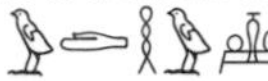, *wdḥw*, "offering table"). At other times it indicates a concept or activity related to it. Determinatives can accompany all sorts of words, as shown on the facing page.

Unfortunately, not every word has a determinative, which is why understanding the phonetic values is important so as to be able to find the word in a vocabulary list or dictionary. For example, prepositions usually do not have a determinative: as in, , *ḥr*, "upon," or , *ẖr*, "with," or , *m*, "in."

There are other words that are normally formed of one sign that both expresses the phonetic value and shows what the word is. So, the sun disc  obviously represents the sun and has the phonetic value *rʿ*. Instead of writing the disc twice, to show that it functioned all as one word, the Egyptians wrote a single vertical stroke beneath it: . The same is true of the words *pr*, "house,"  and *ḥr*, "face," . (Note the difference from the preposition *ḥr* just mentioned, although the preposition can be confusing because it is sometimes written with the stroke.)

And then there are signs that alone write a longer word but do not have a regular phonetic value. Thus,  was explained as a determinative, but because it shows an offering table, it can on its own write a word for "offering table." From examples where the word is fully spelled out , we know the whole word reads *wdḥw*. Other examples appear in Part Two.

HOW TO LOOK UP A WORD: SIGN LISTS AND VOCABULARY

The amateur hieroglyph reader will inevitably have to look up signs and there are some basic rules on how to proceed that will make the task easier. This book uses a standard grouping and numbering of the most common hieroglyphs as refined and compiled by Alan H. Gardiner in his *Egyptian Grammar* (first published in 1927). First, try to identify the different signs and obtain their phonetic values. This will enable you to look up words in a vocabulary list (although you can only do this once you have isolated the word to which each sign belongs; see facing page). To do this, you need a sign list. A very basic sign list (focusing mainly on hieroglyphs used in this book) is included in Part Three. The grammar books cited in Further Reading will contain more detailed lists of the signs. The procedure for using a sign list is summarized in this simple diagram:

IDENTIFY SIGN → LOCATE IN SIGN LIST →

GET POSSIBLE READINGS

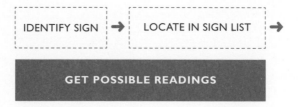

Sign lists are usually divided into twenty-seven sections labelled A to Z and Aa. The signs in each section depict a discrete group of items. For example, section A includes signs that depict men; B gives signs that depict women; N relates to the sky, earth, and water; U covers agriculture, crafts, professions; and so on.

To use a sign list, first locate the individual sign in the list. The notes there give information on what each sign shows and whether it has a phonetic value or mainly acts as a determinative (see pages 31 to 33). Next, assemble the likely phonetic skeleton of the word, and then look up that word in the vocabulary or dictionary.

An example should make this clearer:  is a bird. The sign list reveals that it depicts a swallow and its most common reading is *wr*. The vocabulary list shows those words that begin *wr*. Although time consuming at first, this cross-checking procedure is straightforward and gets quicker and easier with practice.

But what if you cannot work out what a sign shows?  is obviously a man,  a bird, and  a boat, but what about ? To solve this, sign lists are often accompanied by summaries of the more common signs by shape (see pages 144 to 145). A shape list groups signs by shape, giving each sign a code number so that you can look it up in the appropriate category of the sign list. The previous diagram can therefore be modified as follows:

IDENTIFY SIGN → LOCATE IN SHAPE LIST →

GO TO SIGN LIST CATEGORY →

GET POSSIBLE READINGS

A simple example (right) will help to explain the lists. You will see from the shape list that 𓊹 is sign R8, which, from the sign list, is a divine pennant and is usually read *nṯr*. The sign 𓀭 shows a small, seated god, which is often used as a determinative to names and divine words. Look up *nṯr* in the vocabulary and you will find it means "god." *nṯr* is a triliteral sign that frequently stands alone, without phonetic complements or even a determinative, to denote the word "god."

Here is a word with phonetic complements as well (right): it is composed of four signs. You may already recognize the bird 𓅱 as *w* and 𓄿 as *ꜣ*. The second sign is best found in the shape table, where you see it is a fire-drill 𓍑 and reads *ḏꜣ*. Because the following hieroglyph reads *ꜣ*, it is probably a phonetic complement to *ḏꜣ*, thus the word reads *wḏꜣ*. The last sign is a book roll, which is most commonly a determinative of a writing or abstract notion (see page 32). Now that you know how the word reads, look up *wḏꜣ* in the vocabulary and you will find the verb meaning "to be whole, prosperous."

BREAKING UP WORDS AND SENTENCES

In hieroglyphic text there are no gaps between words, nor any punctuation to suggest where parts of sentences start and end. To add to this, the last hieroglyph of a word might look as if it is part of the same group as the first sign of the next word, or two words might be stacked one on top of the other. This is usually the hardest aspect of Egyptian for the beginner, and it is all too easy to divide texts incorrectly, even for more advanced readers.

Think about how you would deal with a sentence in English without word breaks: Thisisashortsentencewithoutanywordbreaks. Can you read it? Of course you can. You are able to do this because you recognize individual words and have some knowledge of English grammar. It's similar with ancient Egyptian—you need a little grammar and to be aware of some common features. Identifying the determinatives (see pages 31 to 33) is a good way to find the ends of individual words and one of the basic ways of breaking up a text. Practice with the example below, which shows how hieroglyphs are broken down:

ḫʿ (kha) + rʿ (re) + m (em) + ȝḫt (akhet)

ROYAL NAMES

WORD ORDER
The royal name "Nebkheperure Tutankhamun" is given below. The divine elements in it, Re and Amun, are written first, at the top of the cartouches, even though they are not read first—an example of honorific transposition (see page 39).

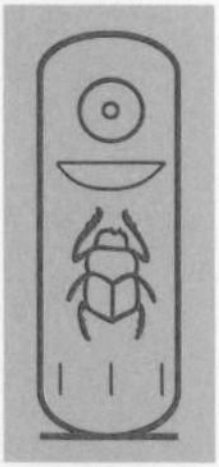

The names of Egyptian kings were frequently inscribed on monuments, and several examples of these texts appear in Part Two. The full royal titulary, or naming convention, evolved over a period of some one thousand years (ca. 3000–2000 BC), but by the Middle Kingdom onward, kings had five names, each of which related to a different part of their identity as rulers. These five names were the "Horus name," the "Two Ladies" or *nebty* name, the "Golden Horus" name, the personal name of the king, and his throne name.

The Horus name, the oldest name of all (from before 3000 BC), was written within a rectangular panel, or *serekh*, with a falcon, *ḥr (hor)*, on the top. This name identifies the king with the deity Horus, son of Osiris, mythical first king of Egypt who became god of the dead. Horus sought revenge for his father's murder and became the next king. The Horus name was particularly common in the first six dynasties (ca. 3000–2181 BC), when it was the main name-form used on official monuments and documents—such as the Peribsen Stela (see page 24) and the Label of King Den (see page 60).

The second name, the *nebty*, used from the First Dynasty on, was less common. It was introduced by the hieroglyph , images of the protective goddesses of Upper and Lower Egypt. *Nebty* (*nbty*) is the dual form (see page 44) of the word *nbt*, "lady," hence the translation "Two Ladies." The third name, the "Golden Horus" name, was rarely used. Its meaning is uncertain, though it probably expresses part of the divinity of the king (in ancient Egyptian, the word "gold" is synonymous with "divine").

From the beginning of the Fourth Dynasty, royal names began to appear inside a "cartouche," an oval loop. The earliest cartouches

THE CARTOUCHE

Two of the names of Egyptian kings were usually enclosed by an oval loop, known as a cartouche, which makes them easy to identify. These loops were thought to resemble early rifle cartridges, hence the name cartouche, from the French for "cartridge."

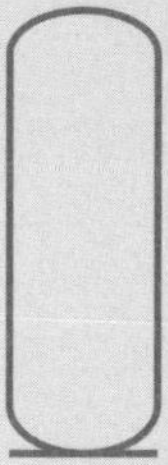

contained the personal name of the king. A second cartouche soon developed, containing the royal throne-name taken by the king at his accession. In the full titulary the throne-name cartouche appears before the personal-name cartouche. The throne name is often compounded with the name of the sun god Re (⊙, *rʿ*), which helps modern-day readers to identify it.

Honorific transposition

The beginner can easily misread the order of signs in a cartouche. Sometimes a name would include within it the name of a king or god (for example, Amenhotep and Tutankhamun include the name of the god Amun; Djedkare includes the name of the god Re). The Egyptians would honor the individual by putting his or her name not in its correct grammatical position, but at the very beginning of the cartouche. Thus the names of Tutankhamun, which read *nb-ḫprw-rʿ twt-ʿnḫ-ỉmn* ("Nebkheperure Tutankhamun," "The Possessor of Forms Is Re, the Living Image of Amun"), are actually written with the signs in the order *rʿ-nb-ḫprw ỉmn-twt-ʿnḫ*—Re and Amun are placed at the beginning of each cartouche (see margin, page 38). Egyptologists call this practice honorific transposition.

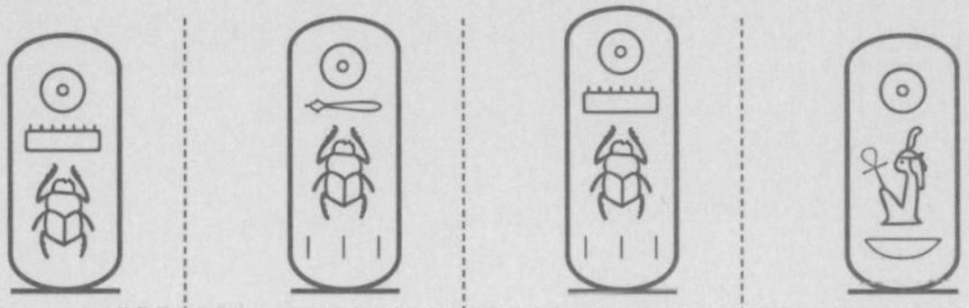

	SIGN ORDER		
rʿ + mn + ḫpr	*rʿ + ʿꜣ + ḫprw*	*rʿ + mn + ḫprw*	*rʿ + mꜣʿt + nb*
	READING ORDER		
mn-ḫpr-rʿ	*ʿꜣ-ḫprw-rʿ*	*mn-ḫprw-rʿ*	*nb-mꜣʿt-rʿ*
	NAME OF KING		
Menkheperre	**Aakheperure**	**Menkheperure**	**Nebmaatre**

The hieroglyphs in the table above, from the Ramesses II king list (see page 62), are examples of honorific transposition. Note that Nebmaatre has a double transposition, with two divine names given (Re and Maat), and so the *nb (neb)*, which should be read first, in fact comes last in the sign order. In addition to the transposition of the proper names of kings and gods, when words simply *describing* kings and gods appeared, they too could be positioned at the beginning of the text. The word for god is *nṯr (netjer)* (𓊹𓀭, often abbreviated to 𓊹) and the word for king is *nswt (nesut)* (𓇓𓏏𓈖, often abbreviated to 𓇓). So, for example, the Egyptian term for "priest" is "servant of the god," and is written with the sign 𓍛 *ḥm (hem)* (an abbreviation for the word "servant") and 𓊹, thus: 𓊹𓍛, *ḥm-nṯr (hem-netjer)*. Similarly, the Egyptian term for "prince" is literally "son of the king," and is written with the sign 𓅭 *zꜣ* (an abbreviation of the word "son" 𓅭𓏤𓀀) and 𓇓, thus: 𓇓𓅭, *zꜣ-nswt (za-nesut)*.

GRAMMAR BASICS

Ancient Egyptian was a living, everyday human language and developed its own versions of most of the common elements of the majority of languages, such as nouns, pronouns, adjectives, prepositions, and verbs. The following are some of the basic features of the grammar that will equip the beginner to read simple texts. (More comprehensive and detailed explanations can be found in the books listed in Further Reading, see pages 156 to 157.)

Nouns and adjectives

A noun is a name for a person, place, object, or living thing. So the Egyptian for "house" is, *pr (per)*, "boat" is *dpt (depet)*, and an Egyptian name might be, *imn-ḥtp*, "Amenhotep." An adjective is a word that is used to describe a noun—for example, "good" as in "good house" (a combination that would have been more common in ancient Egyptian than it is in English). In English, adjectives precede their nouns, but in ancient Egyptian, like French, the adjective usually comes *after* the noun, so "good house" would be, *pr nfr (per nefer)* (literally, "house good").

Gender

Although the English language is gender neutral, most European languages contain masculine and feminine word-forms, and ancient Egyptian is the same. The noun endings clearly reveal whether they are masculine or feminine. The normal feminine ending is, *t*. Thus *dpt* is feminine, as is, *ḫt (khet)*, "thing." Like most languages with more than one gender, when an adjective is placed with a noun, it "agrees" with it in gender, so an adjective describing a feminine

EVERYDAY LANGUAGE

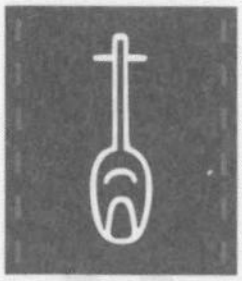

The hieroglyphs that appear in this book come from temples, tombs, and mainly religious contexts. Although they offer some fascinating insights into the life and culture of ancient Egypt—and into the minds of educated Egyptians—the restricted forms of expression used in these formal texts commissioned by a ruling elite are unlikely to mirror the language that was spoken in everyday life by the mass of the largely illiterate population. For example, common words in speech, such as "yes" or "no," appear rarely in such texts. As with languages today, changes to what was written were no doubt driven by developments in speech. It is known for a fact that the quite dramatic changes from Middle to Late Egyptian first made their appearance in the conversational language of daily life, and later began to be written down. Letters, which represent what the writer was thinking, are often difficult texts to follow but they offer a good source of clues to these developments. A second source is provided by captions in Old and Middle Egyptian tombs, which purport to give words being spoken by the actors. Such texts are often difficult to explain gramatically, but then how often do modern English speakers use formal grammar in their daily speech?

noun takes a *t* ending—"good boat" (literally, "boat good") would be , *dpt nfrt (depet neferet)*.

Definite and indefinite articles

Many languages have definite and indefinite articles that accompany nouns—in English these are, respectively, "the" and "a/an." These are not usually found in Middle Egyptian, so the *dpt nfrt* mentioned above could mean "the good boat" or "a good boat"—the best translation would be determined by the context.

Singular, plural, and dual

Nouns also have singular and plural forms (as in, "house," "houses"). The plural in Egyptian uses the ending or , *w*, and a plural noun is usually written with three strokes ||| or ; often the *w* ending is explicitly written, but frequently the three strokes were felt to be all that was needed to express the plural and so the or was omitted, though it should still be written out in transliteration. In the case of a noun that is written with a stroke in the singular (for example, *pr*, "house,"), the three strokes replace the single stroke when the noun is plural. Thus *prw*, "houses," is most commonly written , and much less often or , probably because is the most elegant arrangement. But however it is written, it is still read *prw (peru)*. If the noun is feminine, the plural ending, *w*, occurs before the feminine *t*; so the plural of *dpt* is most often , *dpwt (deput)*, "boats." Adjectives also should agree with the plural noun—*prw nbw (peru nebu)*, "every house/all houses," —though sometimes the distinctive ending is omitted.

Old Egyptian had an attractive way of expressing the plural: instead of using three strokes, it repeated the determinative three times. This is also found sometimes in Middle Egyptian, mostly in temple and tomb inscriptions, so you will find in the texts in this book the plural of 𓊹, *nṯr (netjer)*, as both 𓊹𓏥 and 𓊹𓊹𓊹, *nṯrw (netjeru)*.

As well as the one stroke used to indicate a singular noun, and three strokes a plural, there is also a (not surprisingly) much less common form that indicates "two" of something: the dual. The characteristic ending is *wy* for the masculine and *ty* for the feminine. Thus 𓊹, *nṯr*, "god", 𓊹𓊹, *nṯrwy (netjeruy)*, "two gods."

Possessives

Ancient Egyptian, like English and many other languages, has various ways of expressing possession. For example, "the son of the king" and "his son"—the first uses two nouns and the second a possessive pronoun ("his") and a noun.

Possession of one noun by another noun is achieved in one of two ways in Egyptian. The preposition *n*, 𓈖, can indicate the genitive "of" (it takes the feminine form *nt* when the noun before it is feminine). So *sbꜣ n pr* means usually "the door of the house" and *ḥmt nt ỉmn-ḥtp* means "the wife of Amenhotep." In many cases the link between the two nouns is strong and clear and the Egyptians wrote them next to each other without the *n*; thus *nbt pr* "mistress of the house," or the Egyptian term for "prince" *zꜣ nswt*, "son of the king" (see page 40). Grammarians call these, respectively, the "indirect genitive" and "direct genitive"; Arabic expresses possession in a similar way. (Note that 𓈖 can also indicate the dative "to" or "for," which can confuse the beginner.)

Personal possessives ("his" or "their," for example) are expressed in Middle Egyptian by adding a suffix pronoun to the end of a noun. A suffix pronoun is a personal pronoun that is attached to the end of a noun, verb, or preposition. The table below shows the main forms for Middle Egyptian.

Suffixes work as follows: "His boat" is written by adding the pronoun *·f* to the end of the word for boat: 𓂧𓊪𓏏𓊛𓆑, *dpt·f (depetef)*; "their boat" adds the suffix *·sn*, 𓂧𓊪𓏏𓊛𓋴𓈖𓏥, *dpt·sn (depetsen)*. A raised dot, " · " indicates that a suffix pronoun or some other grammatical element has been attached to a word.

SUFFIX PRONOUNS USED TO INDICATE POSSESSION

HIEROGLYPHS	TRANS-LITERATION	DESCRIPTION	MEANING
𓀀 𓁐	*i*	1st singular (masc., fem.)	my
𓎡	*k*	2nd singular (masc.)	your
𓍿	*ṯ*	2nd singular (fem.)	your
𓆑	*f*	3rd singular (masc.)	his
𓋴	*s*	3rd singular (fem.)	her
𓈖𓏥	*n*	1st plural (masc., fem.)	our
𓍿𓈖𓏥 𓏏𓈖𓏥	*ṯn, tn*	2nd plural (masc., fem.)	your
𓋴𓈖𓏥 𓊃𓈖𓏥	*sn*	3rd plural (masc., fem.)	their

Verbal sentences and verbs

Verbs, which are used to express an action or state of being, are usually one of the hardest parts of any language to master, and this is certainly true of ancient Egyptian. A few basic but important features of verbs are explained below.

• Sentences that in English use the verb "to be"

The verb "to be" is perhaps the most fundamental concept in any system of human communication, but it is also one of the most erratic and irregular verbs in all languages. As in modern Arabic, ancient Egyptian did not need to have an expressed verb such as "am," "is," or "are." Think of the pidgin English "me Tarzan, you Jane." In grammatical English this should be "I am Tarzan, and you are Jane," and it would be poor English not to write the verbs there, but it is acceptable in ancient Egyptian and in colloquial Arabic. These sentence types are called "nonverbal" sentences.

Thus in Arabic, *beiti beitak* translates as "my house is your house." (*Beit* is Arabic for "house," and the endings on it are suffix pronouns that are almost identical to the ancient Egyptian ones.) Here is an Egyptian example:  *ỉnk wḥmw ỉqr (ỉnek wehemu ỉqer)*, "I am an excellent herald" (literally, "I excellent herald"). *wḥmw* is the noun "herald," *ỉqr* the adjective "excellent," following and agreeing with its noun, and *ỉnk* is the first-person singular of another type of pronoun (an independent pronoun), which stands at the beginning of a clause and is a good marker of one of these nonverbal sentences. There are a number of ways nonverbal sentences can be expressed in Egyptian; there are several examples of these sentences in Part Two.

• Infinitives

In English the infinitive is usually considered to be the root form of the verb (for example, "to speak"). The Egyptian infinitive is often very close to the root form of the Egyptian verb, but it also has a construction in which a sentence is started with an infinitive, almost like a caption, or telling a story. For example, , *rdỉt ỉꜣw (redỉt ỉau)*, "giving praise," which might be found both over a figure doing this or the beginning of a hymn to a god: the verb "to give" is , *rdỉ (redỉ)*, and this particular verb makes its (Egyptian) infinitive by adding a *t* (although many do not follow this rule).

• Word order with verbs

In Egyptian the verb usually comes at the beginning of the sentence, and word order relating to verbs is rigid, which is helpful when trying to sort out a sentence. If the subject and object of a verb are both nouns, then the order is *verb-subject-object*. For example, , *mꜣꜣ z zꜣt·f (maa ze zatef)*, "the man sees his daughter" (literally, "sees the man his daughter"): *mꜣꜣ* (verb) + *z* (subject) + *zꜣt·f* (object). But what if the subject of the verb is a pronoun?

• Suffix pronouns as subjects of verbs

Suffix pronouns are used not only as possessives (see page 45) but also as subject pronouns. For example , *ḏd·ỉ (djedỉ)*, "I speak," or , *rḫ·ỉ (rekhỉ)*, "I know." The table on page 48 is a reminder of the form of suffix pronouns, this time giving their meanings when they are used as the subject of a verb. Suffix pronouns are added to the ends of verbs. They take precedence over everything else and cannot exist on their own. For example,

HIEROGLYPHS	TRANS-LITERATION	DESCRIPTION	MEANING
	*ỉ*	1st singular (masc., fem.)	I
	*k*	2nd singular (masc.)	you
	*ṯ*	2nd singular (fem.)	you
	*f*	3rd singular (masc.)	he
	*s*	3rd singular (fem.)	she
	*n*	1st plural (masc., fem.)	we
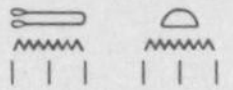	*ṯn, tn*	2nd plural (masc., fem.)	you
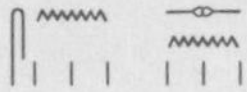	*sn*	3rd plural (masc., fem.)	they

 *ḏd·ṯn rnw·ṯn (djedtjen renutjen)*, "you speak your names," *ḏd* (verb) + *·ṯn* (suffix as subject) + *rnw* (object) + *·ṯn* (suffix as possessive).

Three forms of pronoun were mentioned previously, but only two (suffix and independent pronouns) have been explained so far. The third is the dependent pronoun, which is used mainly as the object of verbs. Unlike the suffix pronoun, it can stand alone and does not need to be attached to a preceding word. But detailed discussion of dependent pronouns really belongs in the next, more advanced stage of study.

NUMBERS AND DATES

Numbers

Basic Egyptian numbers are relatively simple to understand. They bear no relation to the Arabic numerals (0, 1, 2, 3, 4, 5, 6, 7, 8, 9) with which we are familiar, although the ancient Egyptians did count in bases of ten, as we do. Numbers would be written by giving the largest number first and the smallest number last (so, using Arabic numerals as an example, 323 would be written 100 100 100 10 10 III; the Roman equivalent would be CCCXXIII).

In the table on page 50, note how multiple instances of the same character are arranged. This is particularly important for the single digits and tens. Because the signs for one thousand and above are tall, they do not tend to be stacked.

As evident from the table, we do not know the Egyptian names for all the numbers. The numbers one to ten are known (one is *wꜥ*, two is *sn*, three is *ḫmt*, and so on, although four to ten are seldom written out phonetically) and some of the multiples of ten up to one hundred give us readings for them; the readings for powers of ten are given in the table. Although the equivalents for more complicated numbers are known (for example, 16,589 would have been rendered ), it is not known how they would have been pronounced. This is why Egyptologists normally use the Arabic numerals when transliterating a text.

The numbers are usually placed after the noun to which they refer: , *mḥ 1*, literally "cubit one" ("one cubit"). The noun can appear in the singular or plural form: 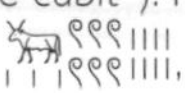, *iḥw 608*, "608 cattle."

NUMBERS TABLE

NUMBER	TRANSLITERATION	HIEROGLYPH
1	*wꜥ*	𓏺
2	*sn*	𓏻
3	*ḫmt*	𓏼
4	*fdw*	𓏽
5	*dỉw*	𓏾
6	*srsw*	𓏿
7	*sfḫ*	𓐀
8	*ḫnmw*	𓐁
9	*psḏw*	𓐂
10	*md*	𓎆
15		𓎆𓏾
20	*? ḏbꜥty ?*	𓎆𓎆
29		𓎆𓎆𓐂
30	*mꜥbꜣ*	𓎆𓎆𓎆
100	*št*	𓍢
105		𓍢𓏾
125		𓍢𓎆𓎆𓏾
1,000	*ḫꜣ*	𓆼
1,100		𓆼𓍢
1,347		𓆼𓍢𓍢𓍢𓎆𓎆𓎆𓎆𓐀
2,000		𓆼𓆼
10,000	*ḏbꜥ*	𓂭
16,589		𓂭𓆼𓆼𓆼𓆼𓆼𓆼𓍢𓍢𓍢𓍢𓍢𓎆𓎆𓎆𓎆𓎆𓎆𓎆𓎆𓐂
100,000	*ḥfn*	𓆐
111,125		𓆐𓂭𓆼𓍢𓎆𓎆𓏾
1,000,000	*ḥḥ*	𓁨

Dates

Dates in the reign of a king were usually presented as follows:  (see pages 90 to 92). The first three signs form a group that means "regnal year." Egyptologists do not agree absolutely on how this should be read, but it is composed of the hieroglyphs 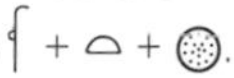.  reads *rnp*, which combines with *t* to form the word for "year," *rnpt (renpet)*. The round sign is *zp (zep)*, "occasion," and so it may mean "year of the occasion" (of the coronation). This is followed by the number of the regnal year, so the example above can be translated as "regnal year three."

An example from a stela of Senwosret III, shows the year and month:

Following the year, the crescent moon with a number below reads *ȝbd* and indicates the month (one to four); the specification of one of the three seasons of the year follows. The seasons were known as Akhet (*ȝḫt*), Peret (*prt*), and Shemu (*šmw*). The date above can therefore be read as: "Regnal year sixteen, third month of Peret," *rnpt zp 16 ȝbd 3 prt (renpet zep 16 abed 3 peret)*.

The three seasons originally corresponded to the inundation (the annual flooding of the Nile river), the appearance of the land from the waters at the end of the inundation, and the hot, growing season. But because the Egyptian year always had 365 days (with no leap year), this calendar gradually got out of step with the real year. This is why the terms "inundation," "winter," and "summer," often found in older publications, have not been included here.

FORMULAS

The "Words Spoken By" formula

Several of the texts in this book are captions over figures of gods with the king, in which the gods are saying what they are doing for the king. These texts, usually in vertical columns in the same orientation as the divine figure, begin with . These signs are highly abbreviated forms (because they are so common) of the verb *ḏd*, , "to speak," and the noun *mdw*, , "words"—it therefore reads *ḏd mdw (djed medu)* and means "speaking words." It is sometimes translated "recitation," or "words spoken." The formula can stand on its own and be immediately followed by the text that is spoken, a sort of "open quotation marks" (though there are no "close" marks), or it can be followed by the preposition *ỉn*, or , "by," and the name of the god who is saying the text. In the latter case, sometimes the actual speech is not given. There are many examples of this among the texts in Part Two.

So now you can recognize the structure of a simple caption such as , *ḏd mdw ỉn wsỉr*, "Words spoken by Osiris."

Expressions used with kings and gods

The name of a king or a god is frequently followed by the word , , or . All read *mry (mery)* and come from the verb *mr (mer)*, "love." These words are called *participles*—effectively adjectives made from a verb—and in this case mean "beloved of." The name of the entity of whom the person is beloved is written before the word *mry*, which is another example of honorific transposition (see pages 39 to 40). Thus reads *mry ỉmn (mery amun)*, "beloved of Amun."

In association with the name of a king, usually after a cartouche, you will see , *dỉ ꜥnḫ (di ankh)*; *dỉ* means "given," so the phrase is "given life." This refers to the fact that the king has been given life by the gods to carry out his role of ruling Egypt. Other items apart from life may be included. For example, , *ḏd (djed)*, "stability," , *wꜣs (was)*, "dominion," and , *snb (seneb)*, "health."

The "Offering" formula

(1) 

(2) 

(3) 

(4) 

Most Egyptian decorated tombs and funerary stelae bear some form of offering formula. The formula is often called the *hetep di nesut* (= "offering" + part of the verb "to give" + "king"), which is usually translated as "an offering which the king gives." The following is an explanation of how it works in translation.

The full formula consists of four basic parts:

(1) the phrase "an offering which the king gives";

(2) the names and epithets of one or more gods (sometimes omitted);

(3) something that will happen as a result of the offering being made (sometimes omitted);

(4) names/titles of the person for whom the offering is made. So the example on page 53 (from the stela on page 100) can be translated as:

"(1) an offering which the king gives

(2) [to] Osiris, lord of Busiris, the Great God, lord of Abydos,

(3) [so that] invocation offerings may be made of thousands of bread, beer, oxen, fowl, alabaster/linen, clothing from the perfect and pure divine offerings on which a god lives

(4) for the honored one, the steward Hetep."

• Notes

(1) is always present. The first signs, , are a usual short form of the word for king, *nswt*, written more fully . This group of signs is placed first due to the "honorific transposition," as explained earlier (see pages 39 to 40). , *ḥtp*, is "offering" and , *di͗*, comes from the verb "to give." All that is required for a basic understanding of this section of the formula is how to recognize the phrase and to know what it means and what can follow.

---

(2) is *wsi͗r*, "Osiris" (without a determinative); is *nb (neb)*, "lord;" is the place name *ḏdw (djedu)*, "Busiris" (the relationship between *nb* and *ḏdw* is a "direct genitive;" see page 44); is the word *nṯr*, "god," here written with the divine determinative, , the adjective *ꜥꜣ*, "great;" is *ꜣbḏw (abdju)*, "Abydos."

---

(3) The hieroglyph shows a combination of the verb *pr*, "to go out," and *ḫrw*, "voice," and is read *prt-ḫrw (peret-kheru)*. It literally means "[so that] the voice might go forth," and is a spoken offering, usually translated as "invocation offering." It is followed by the

offerings that are requested: bread, *t (te)*, ; beer, *ḥnqt (henqet)*, ; oxen, *kꜣ (ka)*, ; fowl, *ꜣpd (aped)*, ; alabaster, or linen, *šs (shes)*, or *sšr (sesher)*, ; clothing, *mnḫt (menkhet)*, . These words are so formulaic that they are just written with one sign each. The following sign is , *ḫꜣ (kha)*, "one thousand," which applies to each of the items just specified. This is followed by the common preposition *m*, which here means "from," and the noun *ḥtp-nṯr (hetep-netjer)*, "divine offering," with the divine hieroglyph put at the front through honorific transposition. These are followed by two adjectives, *nfr (nefer)*, "perfect," and *wꜥb (wab)*, "pure." The last phrase is slightly complicated. It describes the previous offerings, but it can be explained as the verb *ꜥnḫ (ankh)*, "to live," followed by its subject *nṯr (netjer)*, "god," and the word *im (im)*, "thereon," and translated as "on which a god lives."

---

(4) The preposition *n*, , "of, to, for;" the word for a person who has been correctly provisioned for the next life, , *imꜣḫw (imakhu)* (which can be translated "honored one"); and the title and name of the stela owner, "the steward Hetep."

The idea behind the formula was that all things belong to the king and theoretically only he can offer to the gods so that they do something, so Egyptians had to express their wish to obtain offerings this way. Many dozens of expressions can appear as part of (3), such as wishes for traveling well in the next world.

So remember that the signs show you that an offering formula is coming up. Now it is time to start looking at Part Two and some real texts.

II

II

PART TWO

THE HIEROGLYPH DECODER

OIL SLAB

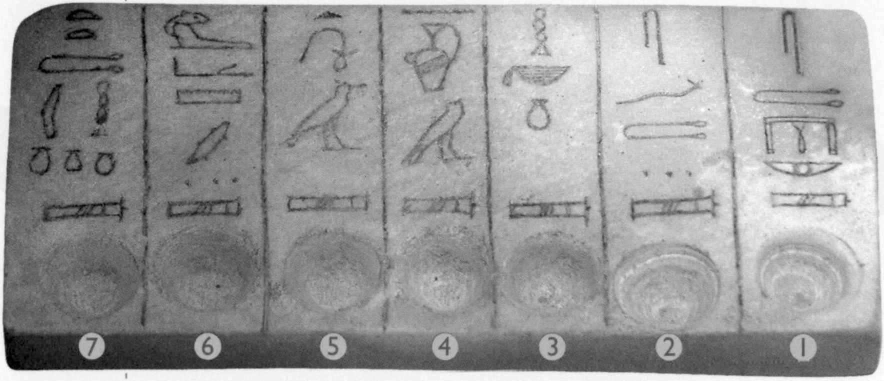

The names of seven, mainly unknown, oils (see page 11) are cut into this stone slab from an Egyptian tomb of the Old Kingdom. Under each is a small depression, which may have held a drop of the oil. The columns are read from right to left and top to bottom.

1 "SETJ-HEB OIL" [UNKNOWN] *sṯ-ḥb (setj-heb)* This word is formed from two single-value signs, *s* and *ṯ*, and a biliteral sign, *ḥb*, , here written with its two component signs; it never exhibits a phonetic complement. The last sign is an oil jar laid on its side (), which acts as a determinative to mark the end of the name of this oil. Note that the jar is written below each of the oils in the slab.

2 "SEFETJ OIL" [UNKNOWN] *sfṯ (sefetj)* The signs for *s* + *f* + *ṯ* plus three dots ooo. One or three dots are often used with oils; they have no phonetic function and are probably serving here as an extra determinative (there is another example in column 6).

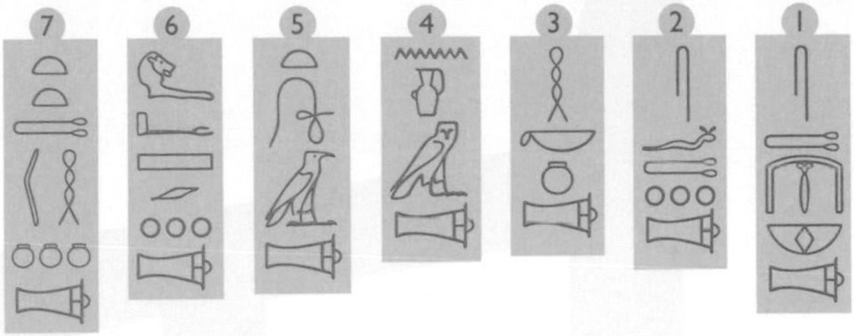

3 "HEKNU OIL" [UNKNOWN] *hknw (heknu)* Two single-letter signs, *h* + *k*, plus the biliteral *nw*.

4 "NEKHENEM OIL" [UNKNOWN] *nḫnm (nekhenem)* The sign *n*, plus a triliteral *ḫnm*, which has the *m* as a phonetic complement.

5 "TUA OIL" [UNKNOWN] *twꜣ (tua)* A single-letter sign, *t*, plus a biliteral *wꜣ*, which has the *ꜣ* as a phonetic complement.

6 "BEST PINE OIL" *ḥꜣtt-ꜥš (hatet-ash)* The first sign is *ḥꜣt*. It works in combination with the two signs at the top of the final column (7) to form the word *ḥꜣtt*, which applies to both columns 6 and 7. The first of the pair of signs, *tt*, serves as a phonetic complement of *ḥꜣt*, so the signs together are read as one word, *ḥꜣtt*, which is used to mean "best of." The hieroglyph 𓆱 is a determinative for items of wood, so the word is *ꜥš*, "pine oil." Thus the whole expression is *ḥꜣtt-ꜥš*, "best pine oil."

7 "BEST TJEHNU OIL" *ḥꜣtt ṯḥnw (hatet tjehenu)* The first two signs belong to *ḥꜣtt* ("best"), applied in the same way here as it does in column 6. The first two signs are 𓍿 + 𓎛; 𓌙 is a throwstick often used with foreign names, and is used here because of the similarity of the sound of this word with the place-name *ṯḥnw*, "Libya." The 𓏌 is repeated three times, like the dots in the other examples. So this oil is *ṯ* + *ḥ* + *nw* (or *nww*), *ḥꜣtt ṯḥnw*, "best tjehnu."

THE LABEL OF KING DEN

Depictions of Egypt's rulers smiting their enemies can be found adorning the gateways of many temples. A similar scene in miniature is shown on this ivory plaque label (note the hole) that was found in the tomb of King Den, the fourth ruler of the First Dynasty, at Abydos (ca. 2940 BC). The appearance of the victim suggests that he is from lands to the east of Egypt, an observation confirmed by the inscription: "The first occasion of smiting the East." Because the

object is from a period early in the development of the Egyptian language and script, not everything is immediately clear, though the picture is helpful. (The action depicted may not refer to an actual event or campaign; it merely reflects a standard way of representing the might of Egypt's ruler.) It is not easy to work out the reading order of these signs; only one sign is not symmetrical, which suggests a place to start. Decoding the signs reveals that they read from left to right and bottom to top.

1

1 "DEN" *dn (den)* The name of the king—his Horus name—is written in a *serekh*, topped by a falcon, above the actors. It is simply composed of two single consonantal hieroglyphs, *d* and *n*—*dn*.

2

2 "SMITING" *sqr (sequer)* This sign is one of those categorized as unclassified. It is transliterated *sqr*, with the phonetic value *sequer*, and it is used here as a verb meaning "to smite." This sign probably faces left, and thus it gives the reader the key to the orientation of the entire text.

3

3 "OCCASION" *zp (zep)* This circle does not have the characteristic dot in the center for the sun (), and it is in fact the pocked circle that represents a threshing floor (). The most common meaning of this word is "time" or "occasion."

4
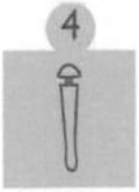

4 "FIRST" *tpy (tepy)* The common adjective meaning "first," represented by an archaic dagger.

5
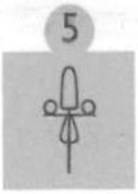

5 "EAST" *i͗ꜣbtt (iabet)* The last sign to the right is a variant on the spear decked out as a standard () and means "east."

THE ABYDOS KING LIST

EMERGENCE
The word *ḫpr* is written with the sign of the dung beetle. It describes the concept of coming into being and can be translated as "manifestation" (as opposite).

In their temples, kings would sometimes be depicted offering to their predecessors, thereby demonstrating their own legitimacy. This section of a now broken list of Ramesses II comes from his temple in Abydos, and dates to ca. 1250 BC. Such lists reflect what the Egyptians at the time wanted to tell the reader, which makes them important for what they omit as much as for what they include. Reading from right to left (because of the direction being faced), the complete hieroglyphs here are rows of six throne-name royal cartouches (see page 38) above the dedicating king, Ramesses II. The four Amarna kings (Akhenaten, Smenkhkare, Tutankhamun, and Ay, ca. 1352–1323 BC) have been omitted because the Amarna heresy period was being expunged from history.

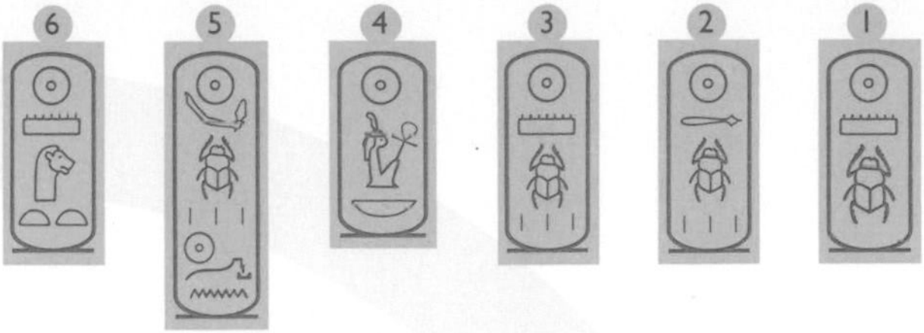

1 "MENKHEPERRE" *mn-ḫpr-rꜥ (men-kheper-re)* The throne name of Thutmose III (r. 1479–1425 BC), which means "Established is the manifestation of Re."

2 "AAKHEPERURE" *ꜥꜣ-ḫprw-rꜥ (aa-kheperu-re)* Note the plural strokes here for what is the throne name of Amenhotep II (r. 1427–1400 BC), which means "Great are the manifestations of Re."

3 "MENKHEPERURE" *mn-ḫprw-rꜥ (men-kheperu-re)* The throne name of Thutmose IV (r. 1400–1390 BC), which means "Established are the manifestations of Re."

4 "NEBMAATRE" *nb-mꜣꜥt-rꜥ (neb-maat-re)* This has a double transposition, with two divine names, so we read *nb-mꜣꜥt-rꜥ*. The throne name of Amenhotep III (r. 1390–1352 BC), which means "Lord of Maat is Re."

5 "DJESERKHEPERURE SETEPENRE" *ḏsr-ḫprw-rꜥ-stp-n-rꜥ (djeser-kheperu-re setep-en-re)* This is a two-part name, which is the throne name of Horemheb (r. 1323–1295 BC) and means "Holy are the manifestations of Re, the Chosen One of Re." (See also page 72.)

6 "MENPEHTYRE" *mn-pḥty-rꜥ (men-pehty-re)* The word *pḥty* is a dual noun (see page 44), meaning "strength." The whole name translates as "Established is the strength of Re," which is the throne name of Ramesses I (r. 1295–1294 BC).

SCRIBES IN MERERUKA'S TOMB

This simple text comes from an Old Kingdom tomb at Saqqara, that of Mereruka, who was the son-in-law of and official to the Sixth-Dynasty pharaoh Teti (2345–2333 BC). The scene shows two men, both scribes, sitting under a canopy and writing with reed pens on what is either a writing board or a sheet of papyrus. The two are part of a scene in which the owner's estates are being recorded. The hieroglyphs consist merely of an administrative title for each man and his name. Ancient Egyptian titles are not easy to decipher because they are often in heavily abbreviated form. It is therefore sometimes difficult for Egyptologists to be certain of their meaning.

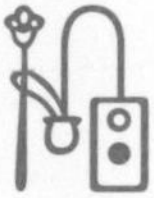

TO WRITE
In addition to being the sign for "scribe," the hieroglyph of the scribal kit indicated the verbs "to write," "to draw," or "to paint."

1 "JUDGE–SCRIBE" *zꜣb zš (zab zesh)* The first two signs of the text on the left give the titles of the man below. The first sign is a jackal, which is a word sign reading *zꜣb*. It has a legal significance and is often translated as "judge." The second sign is also a word sign and represents a palette with two inkwells attached to a pot of water- -the basic writing equipment for a scribe. It reads *zš* and, unsurprisingly, means "scribe."

2 "QARI" *qꜣrỉ (qari)* The rest of the text on the left is the name of the man spelled out with four single phonetic signs, *q + ꜣ + r + ỉ*, or "Qari." The bag is usually the determinative to the group *qꜣr*, the meaning of which is uncertain. The bag is probably placed where it is only for a pleasing arrangement of the signs—something that should always be borne in mind when looking at hieroglyphs.

3 "STEWARD" *ỉmy-r pr (imy-ra per)* The man on the right also has a title. The + is a very compressed writing of a title, which reads *ỉmy-r*—*ỉmy* is derived from the preposition *m* ("in"), and is usually written, but when placed in titles is normally used. is the noun *r* ("mouth"), often written with a stroke after it, but this can be omitted in titles. Literally these two signs read "who is in the mouth," meaning someone who gives orders, which is normally translated as "overseer." (From the later Middle Kingdom, "overseer" is frequently written with the hieroglyph for an animal tongue, which is an attractive graphic wordplay.) The sign with the stroke to the right shows a house, and reads *pr*, meaning "house." The full title is therefore "overseer of the house," often translated as "steward."

4 "[OF] NYANKHKHNUM" *n-ꜥnḫ-ḫnmw (ny-ankh-khenemu)* The name has three parts (+ *ꜥnḫ + n*). The ram represents the creator god Khnum, *ḫnmw* in transliteration. The *ꜥnḫ* ("ankh") may be familiar (see page 30), and *n* is the preposition "of". The name is normally read as above (although the full explanation for this is complex), with the divine name transposed later, as is usual.

NEFERTARI PLAYING SENET

Queen Nefertari plays *senet*. Often depicted on tomb walls, the game was a symbol of the journey of the deceased after death. *Senet* sets were sometimes placed in burial tombs to aid the dead on this journey. The game is not mentioned in the text, which reads, "The Osiris, great wife of the king, lady of the two lands, Nefertari, beloved one of Mut, true of voice before Osiris, the great god."

1 "THE OSIRIS, GREAT WIFE OF THE KING" *wsir ḥmt nswt wrt (usir hemet nesut weret)* The first word is *wsỉr*, "Osiris" (see page 72). is shorthand for *nswt* ("king"). At upper left, (rendered a little differently from usual) represents a well with water and has the value *ḥm*. It is followed by the feminine ending *t—ḥmt* means "wife." So this group of three signs reads *ḥmt nswt* (*nswt* is placed in front as an honorific transposition) and means "wife of the king." The swallow, , at the bottom of the column reads *wr*, and also has a feminine ending; *wr* is an adjective meaning "great," and the *t* makes it agree with the word *ḥmt*. The whole phrase means "great wife of the king," the standard Egyptian term for the king's principal consort.

2 "LADY OF THE TWO LANDS" *nbt tȝwy (nebet tawy)* At the top of the second column is *nbt*, not another adjective but the word for "lady." The two horizontal signs mean "land" and read *tȝ*; two of these signs together read *tȝwy* and mean the "two lands" (a reference to Upper and Lower Egypt).

3 "NEFERTARI, BELOVED ONE OF MUT" *nfrt-iry mrt-n-mwt (nefret-iry meret-en-mut)* The first part of the cartouche spells out *nfrt-ỉry*, the famous Nefertari. A description follows of a deity by whom she is loved. The vulture reads *mwt* ("Mut"), and as so often the small phonetic complement *t* is written below its breast. Mut is the consort of Amun of Thebes and a major divinity in that city. Instead of *mry*, this text writes the feminine form *mrt*, and there is also a genitive *n*, so it is read *mrt n mwt*, "the beloved one of Mut."

4 "TRUE OF VOICE BEFORE OSIRIS, THE GREAT GOD" *mȝʿ-ḫrw ḫr wsỉr nṯr ʿȝ (maa-kheru kher usir netjer aa)* The last two columns read "true of voice before Osiris the great god" (explained in more detail on page 73). But note that this oar (top) is flat instead of vertical, and there is a phonetic complement with the column . Normally *mȝʿ-ḫrw* would show the feminine form *mȝʿt-ḫrw* because the person referred to is female, but not in this instance.

THE GODDESS MAAT

Recognizable by the feather, the goddess Maat is the embodiment of the concept *maat*, which means "truth" or "justice." Until its removal in the nineteenth century, this relief was part of the tomb of Sety I in the Valley of the Kings. The caption reads, "Maat, daughter of Re, mistress who is foremost of the land of Iugeret."

1 "MAAT" *mꜣꜥt (maat)* The orientation shows that the reader starts from the left. The first sign, reading *mꜣ*, is followed by two phonetic signs, *ꜥ* and *t*, and then a small, seated woman (with a feather on her head) holding an *ankh*. This figure is the determinative; the sign can stand on its own for the goddess's name.

2 "DAUGHTER OF RE" *zꜣt rꜥ (zat re)* The sun disc is the name *rꜥ* (the sun god Re). The pintail duck reads *zꜣ*, and the semi-circle is the feminine suffix *t*. A graphic peculiarity of Egyptian is that a very small sign—especially the ending *t*—can sometimes fill up the vacant space under the breast of a bird instead of occupying the logical position behind the bird. This happens particularly when the next sign fits neatly into that space, as here. So this word should read *zꜣ + t = zꜣt*, "daughter" (and here, "daughter of Re").

3 "MISTRESS" *ḥnwt (henut)* Looking up in the sign list gives the value *ḥnwt*, which is confirmed by the adjacent phonetic complements *ḥ* and *t*. The meaning of the word *ḥnwt* is "mistress." (It is next to the picture of a goddess, which could be thought of as the determinative to the word *ḥnwt*.) Usually when a goddess is called *ḥnwt*, a location is specified, so this must now be found.

4 "WHO IS FOREMOST OF THE LAND OF IUGERET" *ḥrt-tp tꜣ n iwgrt (heret-tep ta en iugeret)* The signs combine to form the phrase *ḥrt-tp*, meaning "who is foremost of." This is the feminine form of the basic sign *ḥrt-tp*, made so by the addition of the *t* to agree with Maat, to whom it refers. The next three signs, are made from, which reads *tꜣ*, with the single stroke | and a determinative of a piece of land; together they mean "land." The next sign is, commonly the genitive "of," thus giving "land of." The remaining signs form the group, determined with the sign, which is used to indicate a desert or foreign land. The signs spell out *iwgrt*, "Iugeret," a name for the necropolis or the realm of the dead.

THE KING AND A GODDESS

The central section of this wall painting from the tomb of King Horemheb (ca.1323–1295 BC) shows the ruler wearing the distinctive *nemes* headdress. Facing him is a goddess, wearing a horned headdress. (She cannot be identified with certainty from this as several deities have similar headwear.) The inscriptions reveal the two figures as Horemheb and the goddess Hathor (see page 73). The script above Hathor's head reads, "Words spoken by Hathor foremost of Thebes, mistress of all the gods, lady of heaven."

Opposite Hathor, two cartouches form the major elements of the inscription (facing left) above the king. One is the ruler's throne name, or praenomen, and the other is his birth name, or nomen. The whole text reads, "The Osiris, the king, Djeserkheperure Setepenre, son of Re, Horemheb Meryenamun, true of voice before Osiris the great god."

1 "WORDS SPOKEN BY" *ḏd mdw in (djed medu in)* This begins with , recognizable as the "Words Spoken" formula, *ḏd mdw* (see page 52), with the preposition *in*, "by," which is usually followed by the name of the deity who is speaking.

2 "HATHOR" *ḥwt-ḥr (hat-hor)* This sign is an enlarged version of , *ḥwt*, with a falcon (Horus, *ḥr*). The sign list reveals that is *ḥwt-ḥr*, the transliterated form of the name of the goddess Hathor. Because Hathor is a deity, the next phrase is likely to be an attribute, or similar (Maat was the "daughter of Re"; see page 69).

3 "WHO IS FOREMOST OF THEBES" *ḥr-tp wꜣst (her-tep waset)* The that follows Hathor is usually written ; it is the phrase *ḥr-tp*, "who is foremost of," and in this example the artist did not put it in the feminine form. The next sign is a special version of (*wꜣs*). The *t* after it gives the word *wꜣst*, the name of the ancient city of Thebes. It has two determinatives, , a grid of irrigated land, which can be used with geographical terms, and , a determinative used with place-names—a stylized town with a large crossroads in the middle. So Hathor is "foremost of Thebes."

4 "MISTRESS OF ALL THE GODS" *ḥnwt nṯrw nbw (henut netjeru nebu)* The word *ḥnwt* may be familiar from page 69, and the sign repeated three times after it is an old-fashioned way of writing a plural *nṯrw* for "gods." The basket above the horns also has a plural, this time with the three strokes, and it is an adjective belonging to *nṯrw*; it reads *nbw*, and *nṯrw nbw* means "all the gods."

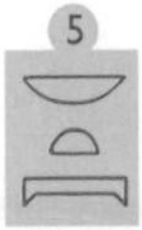

5 "LADY OF HEAVEN" *nbt pt (nebet pet)* Although this next word also has the *nb* sign in it, this is not the *nb* meaning "all," but the feminine form *nbt* of the noun *nb*, "lord, master"—therefore "lady" or "mistress." The following sign, , most commonly reads *pt*, "sky, heaven" and describes what she is lady of, thus "lady of heaven," a direct genitive (see page 44).

6

6 "THE OSIRIS" *wsỉr (usir)* The next hieroglyphs spell out a couple of words that are very common, but are not easy to look up. These two signs normally read *ỉr* and *st*. They are placed together here to write the word *wsỉr*, which means "Osiris." Although Osiris is the name of the god of the dead (see page 116), the word is also used generally for a deceased person; sometimes it is written with the divine determinative, but often it is not.

7

7 "THE KING" *nswt (nesut)* The next three signs are read in the order + + and read *nswt*, the Egyptian word for "king." This is often abbreviated to because it is so common—an important point for beginners to remember.

8

8 "DJESERKHEPERURE SETEPENRE" *ḏsr-ḫprw-rʿ stp-n-rʿ (djeser-kheperu-re setep-en-re)* This is the two-part throne name, or praenomen, of Horemheb and means "Holy are the manifestations of Re, the Chosen One of Re," as seen previously in the Abydos king list (see pages 62 to 63).

9

9 "SON OF RE, HOREMHEB MERYENAMUN" *zꜣ rʿ ḥr-m-ḥb mry-n-ỉmn (za re hor-em-heb mery-en-amun)* This second cartouche displays the king's birth name, or nomen, though it is accompanied by two signs before it, which should be recognized: *zꜣ* and *rʿ* ("son of Re")—a standard epithet for the king since the Fourth Dynasty. The first four signs are not part of his actual name; one, the sign , may be familiar from the section on formulas (see page 52) where it is given as the word *mry* ("beloved"), usually preceded by the name of a god. A quick check of shows that it reads *ỉmn*, the god Amun, and the sign is here the genitive *n*, so this king is *mry-n-ỉmn* ("beloved of Amun"). The king's personal name is written quite concisely: + + , *ḥr + m + ḥb*, *ḥr-m-ḥb*, Horemheb, which actually means "Horus is in festival." The epithet of Horemheb is here transposed before the name, but we believe that it would have been read after the name.

10 "TRUE OF VOICE BEFORE OSIRIS THE GREAT GOD" *mꜣꜥ-ḫrw ḥr wsỉr nṯr ꜥꜣ (maa-kheru kher usir netjer aa)* This begins with the signs for the adjective *mꜣꜥ* ("true"). The next sign is the oar , which here has the phonetic value *ḫrw*—the *w* is thus a phonetic complement. This word means "voice," and the expression *mꜣꜥ-ḫrw* literally means "true of voice." This is a reference to judgment after death (see page 114), when a man who was permitted to go into the next world was called "true of voice." The god who presides over the judgment is *wsỉr*, "Osiris," here with a determinative . Before this name the signs + form the preposition *ḥr* ("before"). The last hieroglyphs are , *nṯr*, and , which reads *ꜥꜣ*. This has the abstract determinative , and is an adjective meaning "great," thus "great god." This is a common epithet of Osiris but it was used for a range of gods.

10

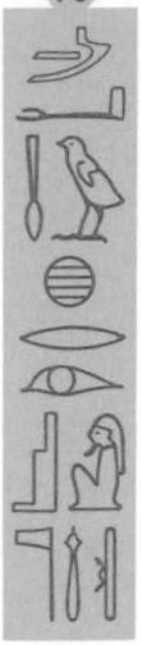

HATHOR, "MANSION OF HORUS"

A universal cow goddess, the mother of the king, and an important protective divinity for women, Hathor (*ḥwt-ḥr*, which means "Mansion of Horus") is a complex deity. Her principal cult center was at Dendera, between Thebes and Abydos. Because she can be shown in many forms, particularly as a cow or as a woman wearing cow's horns (which is also used for other goddesses), it is important to check the hieroglyphs carefully. Hathor was also considered "mistress of the West," the direction associated with the afterlife, reflecting her role as a funerary goddess.

THE SLAB OF NEFRETIABET

This stone slab stela contains elements (such as a "linen list") that make it likely to date from the Fourth Dynasty. It is from the Giza tomb of an important woman, and the offering texts on it are simple. To the left is a seated figure, the tomb owner, with her name and title above; in the center, at the top, is a two-part offering list; in the center, at the bottom, there are offerings above and below the table (the latter are not examined opposite); and occupying the right side is what is believed to be an ideal "linen list."

1 "THE KING'S DAUGHTER, NEFRETIABET" *zȝt nswt nfrt-ỉȝbt (zat nesut nefret-iabet)* is the abbreviation for *nswt*, "king" (often put at the front, though it should be read second), and *zȝt* is the word for "daughter," giving *zȝt nswt*, or "king's daughter." The name has two principal signs, and , each with a *t* below. The *t* below *nfr* is a feminine ending; the second *t* is the phonetic complement of the word *ỉȝbt*. The woman's name is therefore *nfrt-ỉȝbt*, "Nefretiabet." "King's daughter" was not necessarily literal but an Old Kingdom term of honor and rank given to some women.

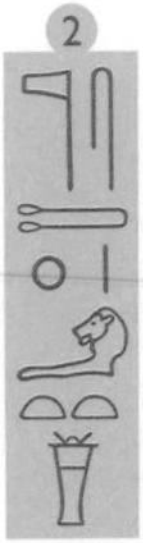

2 "INCENSE, BEST OIL" *snṯr ḥȝtt mrḥt (senetjer hatet merhet)* The offering items are written vertically; the divisions between them are not marked by dividing lines. In the top row, the first word is , which is *snṯr*, "incense." (Oddly, the *s* is written after the *nṯr* sign—perhaps the sculptor thought he should apply honorific transposition to the *nṯr* sign, as he knew it could mean "god.") , *ḥȝtt*, means "best," referring to the small oil jar that is positioned below these signs. The most common oil is , *mrḥt*, so the jar may be a short writing of this word.

3 "CAROB BEAN" *wꜥḥ (wah)* In the lower row, the first signs are , which read *wꜥḥ*, "carob bean" (though the signs read *ḥ-w-ꜥ*). may be below the other two to fit more neatly in the column (and a bird with a space below the breast often goes after instead of in front of a more vertical sign). is a determinative; the use of a moon sign in this word might be something to do with the similarity of the sound of this word with *ỉꜥḥ*, "moon."

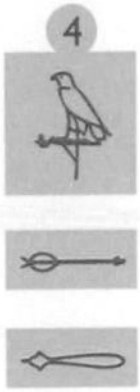

4 "LINEN" *ỉdmy sšr ꜥȝ (idmey sesher aa)* The area on the right is thought to be a "linen list"—valuable pieces of linen would form part of an ideal burial in the Old Kingdom. The hawks at the top are thought to represent *ỉdmy* linen, the signs under the arrow in the middle *sšr* linen, and those under the *ꜥȝ* sign, *ꜥȝ* linen; the *ỉdmy* is probably red linen, but the exact nature of the other two is unclear.

THE TOMB OF RAMESSES I

The tomb of Ramesses I (r. 1292–1290 BC) contains colorful paintings that have survived well. The inscriptions reveal that the three figures—in a pose signifying "jubilation" (exemplified by)—represent two groups: "Words spoken by the spirits of Pe; they rejoice for Horakhty and their son, the Osiris, the king Menpehtyre, son of Re, Ramesses" and "Words spoken by the spirits of Nekhen; they make rejoicing for the lords of eternity."

1 "WORDS SPOKEN BY" *ḏd mdw ỉn (djed medu in)* This column begins with *ḏd mdw ỉn*, familiar to readers of hieroglyphs as the "Words Spoken By" formula (see page 52).

2 "SPIRITS OF PE" *bȝw p (bau pe)* The sign for *bȝw*, or "spirits," is followed by a place name , which should be recognizable as such from the determinative ⊗. It reads *p* (ignore the two strokes), the Egyptian name for the ancient Delta city of Buto, the cult center of the Lower Egyptian deity Wadjet (the cobra ). These are therefore the "spirits of Pe" (see page 79).

3 "THEY REJOICE" *ḥny·sn (heneysen)* The first word is *ḥny*, and from the determinative , the reader should expect an association with rejoicing; indeed, it is a form of the verb *ḥnw*, "to rejoice." With the suffix pronoun *·sn* ("they"), the signs read "they rejoice."

4 "FOR HORAKHTY" *n ḥr-ȝḫty (en hor-akhty)* The here is the dative *n*, "for," followed by a falcon, *ḥr*, "Horus." The two  behind the bird represent the two horizons and are most commonly used in the name of two gods, one of whom is *ḥr-ȝḫty* "Horakhty." *ȝḫty* is the dual form of the singular noun *ȝḫt*, "horizon" (often written  when used in other contexts). Horakhty therefore means "Horus of the two horizons," a fitting name for an important sky deity.

5 "[AND] THEIR SON, THE OSIRIS, THE KING" *zȝ·sn wsỉr nswt (sasen usir nesut)* The next hieroglyph is , with a stroke, which reads *zȝ*, and usually means "son"; it is written here without a determinative, which is not unusual. Note the suffix pronoun *·sn*, so this means "their son." To determine the relationship of this to the rest of the sentence, "and" probably has to be added after "Horakhty." (It is common for ancient Egyptian to list multiple items without conjunctions.) The spirits are therefore praising both Horakhty and their son. The cartouches in the next two columns reveal to the reader that "their son" is the king. The first cartouche

6

is the throne name (see below) and before it are three signs, , , and . If you look up in the sign list, you will see that   is an alternative writing of *wsỉr* ("Osiris") and is an abbreviation for *nswt* ("king"), so this reads "the Osiris, the king," indicating that the ruler is thought of here as deceased.

---

6 "MENPEHTYRE" *mn-pḥty-rʿ (men-pehty-re)* Ramesses I's throne name was spelled differently on the Abydos king list (see page 63); whereas there the was accompanied by two s, here it stands alone. But it should still be read as if it were a dual form, *pḥty*, *mn-pḥty-rʿ*. Again, this shows the flexibility of hieroglyphic writing—the scribe may have felt he had insufficient room to write two s.

7

---

7 "SON OF RE" *zꜣ rʿ (za re)* As in the earlier inscription (see page 77), is the sign for "son," but is accompanied here by the sun disc , *rʿ* ("the god Re"), and therefore reads "son of Re."

8

---

8 "RAMESSES" *rʿ-ms-sw (ra-mes-su)* The second cartouche almost certainly has to be the personal name Ramesses. The ("the god Re") is given at the top, but the sign should be read where it stands rather than being transposed to the end of the name. This is followed by , plus the phonetic complement , and , with the complement . These two groups are transliterated *ms* and *sw* respectively, giving the whole name *rʿ-ms-sw*, "Ramessu," from which the Greek form, Ramesses, is derived.

9

---

9 "WORDS SPOKEN BY" *ḏd mdw ỉn (djed medu in)* Skipping a column that begins "true of voice," a second inscription is signaled by use of the "Words Spoken by" formula, *ḏd mdw ỉn* (see page 52), indicating that a name will follow.

10

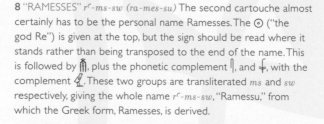

---

10 "SPIRITS OF NEKHEN" *bꜣw nḫn (bau nekhen)* Balancing the text to the right, *bꜣw*, "spirits," is followed by a place name . The sign writes the name of the town *nḫn*, "Nekhen [Hierakonpolis]." The is therefore a phonetic complement and these characters are "the spirits of Nekhen." Nekhen, like Pe, is a very old city, the home of Nekhbet, the protective goddess of Upper Egypt.

11

11 "THEY MAKE REJOICING" *ỉry·sn hnw (irysen henu)* Next is another verb with a suffix pronoun as subject. The verb is *ỉr* (here *ỉry*), "to do/make," so *ỉry·sn* is "they make." The verb needs an object indicating what is being done or made, and it is *hnw*, at the top of the last column—a noun related to the verb *hny* in the second column (see page 77), "to rejoice."

12

12 "FOR THE LORDS OF ETERNITY" *n nbw nḥḥ (en nebu neheh)* The next word is *nbw*, which could, of course, be an adjective, "all," agreeing with *hnw*, or it could be "lords," without a determinative. Only practice in the language will confirm which is the best option here—but look at the next word (under the arm of the hawk-headed figure), which is . This word is tricky because it is a common form of the full word  (*nḥḥ*, "eternity"). As the word *nḥḥ* would otherwise not belong to anything, it is better to read *nbw* with *nbw* as "lords of eternity."

THE SPIRITS OF PE AND NEKHEN

The spirits of Pe and Nekhen are thought to represent the semi-mythical rulers of the predynastic states of the north and the south, and were seen as protective ancestors of the reigning king. Buto and Hierakonpolis, ancient major cities of Lower and Upper Egypt (the "Two Lands"), have yielded much material from the earliest periods. The temples of the protective goddesses of the two lands (Wadjet and Nekhbet) were located at these sites.

THE WHITE CHAPEL OF SENWOSRET I

The limestone chapel of King Senwosret I (r. 1919–1875 BC) was discovered in the filling of a gateway of the temple of Amun at Karnak. (Egyptian monuments were often reused as building materials in this way.) The chapel may originally have been a barque shrine, where the divine boat containing the image of Amun would have rested when not on procession. The pillars and walls are decorated with a variety of scenes, mostly of the king before the god Amun. The selected inscriptions from two columns read, "Horus Ankhmesut, Two Ladies Ankhmesut, Son of Re, Senwosret, Perfect God, Lord of the Two Lands, Lord of Cult Action(s)."

1 "HORUS ANKHMESUT" *ḥr ꜥnḫ-mswt (her ankh-mesut)* The first of the two selected columns begins with the king's royal names. The Horus name (see page 38) in the *serekh* reads *ꜥnḫ-mswt*, "Ankhmesut."

2 "TWO LADIES ANKHMESUT" *nbty ꜥnḫ-mswt (nebty ankh-mesut)* Next is , which marks the *nebty* name (see page 38). The four hieroglyphs that follow the *nebty* name match the Horus name, "Ankhmesut;" in the Middle Kingdom (ca. 2016–1650 BC) it was not unusual for kings to use the same Horus and *nebty* names.

3 "SON OF RE" *zꜣ rꜥ (za re)* The top of the next column displays the title, *zꜣ rꜥ*, "son of Re," which usually comes before the cartouche.

4 "SENWOSRET" *z-n-wsrt (ze-en-usret)* The name in the cartouche can sometimes be difficult to decipher. The first sign is , *wsr*; the *s* and *r* are phonetic complements and should not be read again. The next sign, *t*, is the feminine ending, giving *wsrt*, "Wosret" —a Theban goddess, who may have been a consort of Amun (preceding Mut). Then and : *z* is the word for "man" and *n* is the genitive, so the divine name has probably been honorifically transposed to read *z-n-wsrt*, "Senwosret," meaning "man of Wosret."

5 "PERFECT GOD" *nṯr nfr (netjer nefer)* The signs in this first epithet of the king are readily recognized as *nṯr nfr*, "perfect god." The adjective *nfr* also means "good," but in religious contexts it is usually better translated as "perfect."

6 "LORD OF THE TWO LANDS" *nb tꜣwy (neb tawy)* The signs in the second epithet represent *nb tꜣwy*, "lord of the two lands," an important reference to the king's political and religious roles in maintaining the unity of the realm (see pages 108 to 109).

7 "LORD OF CULT ACTION(S)" *nb ỉr ḫt (neb ir khet)* The first sign is *nb*, "lord," plus the signs + + . is part of the verb *ỉr*, "to do," and means "doing" or "who does"; the other two signs form the word *ḫt*, "thing," thus "lord who does thing(s)." This strange epithet is thought to mean something like "lord of cult action(s)," referring to the role of the king as high priest of every cult.

NECTANEBO WITH THOTH

This granite block from Abydos shows the king Nectanebo I (r. 380–362 BC) presenting the god Thoth with a statuette of the goddess Maat (see page 68), representing the fact that the ruler was obliged to make offerings to the gods who protected Egypt. Although Thoth was usually depicted as an ibis or an ibis-headed man, he is shown here as a baboon. His cult center was Khemenu (Hermopolis), with smaller centers elsewhere. Thoth is a patron deity of scribes, as well as of wisdom and magic. He was also a moon god, which is the form taken here (note the moon disc and crescent). The main selected inscriptions here read, "Nectanebo; Djehuty, controller of the gods, the great god, lord of heaven; offering Maat to his father who makes for him 'given life.'"

1 "NECTANEBO" *nḫt-nb·f (nakht-nebef)* The first word of the left-hand cartouche is *nḫt* written with 𓈖, plus the biliteral sign 𓆱, *ḫt*, and all the phonetic complements written out; because it means "strong" it has the determinative (𓂡) showing physical activity or force. The small recumbent lion (actually almost

certainly a sphinx) is occasionally used to write *nb* ("lord"), here with the possessive *·f* ("his lord"). The name in Egyptian writing is *nḫt-nb·f*, or "Nakhtnebef," transcribed by the Greeks as Nectanebo.

2

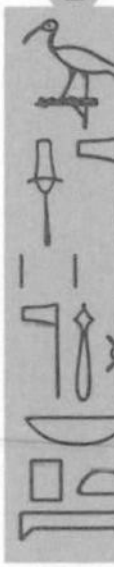

2 "DJEHUTY, CONTROLLER OF THE GODS, THE GREAT GOD, LORD OF HEAVEN" *ḏḥwty ḫrp nṯrw nṯr ꜥꜣ nb pt (djehuty kherep netjeru netjer aa neb pet)* Above Thoth's head is his name and epithet. At the top is the ibis hieroglyph , often used to express his name. This sign reads *ḏḥwty*, "Djehuty" ("Thoth" is Greek). Epithets follow, among them, *nṯrw* ("gods"), and the sign before it ( ) can be read either *sḫm*, "powerful one," or *ḫrp*, "controller." The two words are joined by a direct genitive, "of the gods." The word *nṯr* appears again in the next column, with the adjective *ꜥꜣ*, "the great god," and the hieroglyphs *nb pt*, "lord of heaven"; here *pt* is written fully phonetically, not just with the sign .

3

3 "OFFERING MAAT TO HIS FATHER WHO MAKES FOR HIM 'GIVEN LIFE'" *ḥnk mꜣꜥt n it·f ir n·f di ꜥnḫ (henek maat en itef ir enef di ankh)* The first sign does not have any phonetic complements and is thus a word on its own. Two readings are possible, *ḥnk* and *ḏrp*, both meaning "offer," but we know from fuller examples, such as , that *ḥnk* is correct here. The next word was seen on page 69 (above the figure of the goddess Maat holding an *ankh*). The that follows is the dative "to," and the person to whom it is offered is called . This is the most common writing for *it*, "father" (sometimes but not always with a determinative) and despite the fact that there is no *f* in the spelling, the is always a part of the word. As the is there, when the Egyptians come to write *it·f*, "his father," they often do not bother to write the again. The following is the verb *ir*, "to do/make," and means "who makes," while the is the dative, followed by the suffix , "for him." The last two signs are a set expression used in relation to the king, reading *di ꜥnḫ* (see page 53); the whole phrase, *ir n·f di ꜥnḫ*, means "who makes for him (the state of) 'given life.'"

SENWOSRET III OFFERING TO THE GODS

Egyptian temples were usually adorned with scenes of the king making offerings to the gods. The relief shown below—with two almost symmetrical scenes on either side of a central axis—is on a limestone lintel that spanned a doorway in the temple dedicated to Montu at Medamud in Upper Egypt. The king (center), beneath the

ANKH
The *ankh* is the standard sign used to write "life," "to live," "alive," and "living." Gods are often shown grasping *ankh* signs and also presenting them to a king.

protective winged sun discs, can be identified from the cartouche (see page 86) above his head: Senwosret III (r. 1878–1839 BC). Above the falcon-headed god on either side are passages of inscription that begin with the common formula *ḏd mdw*. The main texts read, "I have given to you all life and dominion" and "I have given you all health and all joy, like Re." The god is kilted and holds an *ankh* sign and a scepter; the hieroglyphs above his plumed solar headdress with double uraeus confirm him as Montu.

1 "KHAKAURE" *ḫꜥ-kꜣw-rꜥ (kha-kau-re)* The obvious first task when presented with an inscription of this kind is to attempt to identify the king's name, which is written inside the cartouche. This cartouche is written *rꜥ* + *ḫꜥ* + *kꜣw*—the triplicated sign is a writing of the plural of *kꜣ*, "*ka*-soul." (*Ka* was the individual's creative life energy, which remained in existence after the body's death.) As is usual, the *rꜥ* element is placed first, but it should be read last, so the name is *ḫꜥ-kꜣw-rꜥ*, or "Khakaure" (meaning "The souls of Re appear"), which is the throne name of the king better known as Senwosret III of the Twelfth Dynasty. Senwosret undertook reorganization of the administration of Egypt and conducted limited campaigns in the Near East. In Nubia he consolidated Egypt's hold on the area south of the Second Cataract (in modern-day Sudan).

2 "WORDS SPOKEN" *ḏd mdw (djed medu)* The traditional offering formula, "Words Spoken," appears next (see page 52).

3 "I HAVE GIVEN TO YOU" *dỉ·n·(ỉ) n·k (dieni enek)* The first sign here, , reads *dỉ* and is part of the verb *rdỉ*, "give." The formula here is actually an old one, and the *dỉ·n* inscribed is short for *dỉ·n·ỉ* "I have given" (the before the subject marks the past tense); sometimes the suffix of the first person *·ỉ* is dropped (this could be because it was not sounded strongly). The and are the dative *n·k*, "to you," and so this common phrase reads, *dỉ·n·(ỉ) n·k* "I have given to you," and is followed by the object of the verb (what has been given), as explained below.

4 "ALL LIFE AND DOMINION" *ꜥnḫ wꜣs nb (ankh was neb)* The specification + + consists of *ꜥnḫ* ("life") and *wꜣs* ("dominion"), with the adjective *nb* ("all") applying to both—this therefore reads "all life and dominion." Note that only one of the "Words Spoken," or *ḏd mdw*, formulas is read—sometimes the Egyptians wrote the formula above every column in a recitation by a god, as by Montu here.

5

5 "WORDS SPOKEN" *ḏd mdw (djed medu)* The speech uttered by the god on the left-hand side of the lintel begins with the standard "Words Spoken" formula.

6 "I HAVE GIVEN TO YOU" *dỉ·n.(ỉ) n·k (dieni enek)* (see 3).

7

7 "ALL HEALTH [AND] ALL JOY, LIKE RE" *snb nb ꜣwt-ỉb nb mỉ rꜥ (seneb neb aut-ib neb mi re)* The two *nb* signs are the adjective "all," following nouns. The first word, , spells *snb*, "health," and is one of the few three-letter words that does not use either a biliteral or triliteral sign. The next sign, , reads *ꜣw* and has the feminine ending *t*, hence *ꜣwt*. It is followed by , the noun *ỉb*, which on its own means "heart." Together this gives a two-word noun, *ꜣwt-ỉb*, "joy." The sign reads *mỉ* and is a preposition meaning "like." A preposition comes before its noun, so where is that noun? The sign before the noun is the sun disc *rꜥ*, and this must be the name of the god Re transposed before the *mỉ*.

8

8 "MONTU, LORD OF THEBES" *mnṯw nb wꜣst (montju neb waset)* The name of the god is above the plumes on his head: + + , giving *mnṯw*, "Montu." Below the is the word *nb*, "lord," and a place-name *wꜣst*, "Thebes," hence "Montu, lord of Thebes." Montu was probably the original local god of Thebes before becoming subordinated to Amun during the Twelfth Dynasty, and was usually shown as he is here, a man with a falcon's head. During the Middle Kingdom era (ca. 2016–1650 BC) he began to be venerated as a war deity, following the reunification of Egypt after the instability of the first Intermediate Period. This reverence reached its height under the New Kingdom pharaohs of the Eighteenth Dynasty. It should be noted that there is no hieroglyphic determinative to the signs for Montu; the picture of the god below probably carries out this function. This is an example of the wonderful interplay between text and image in Egyptian art.

11

THE TOMB OF ROY

JACKAL
Only when recumbent did the hieroglyph of this dog-like animal specify Anubis, the jackal-headed figure closely associated with mummification and the events in the Hall of Judgment (see pages 114 to 117).

In the tomb of Roy at Thebes, a scene shows a priest dressed as the embalmer god Anubis (above his ears is written *r-y* "Roy" [1]). To the left are two more priests, one pouring a purifying libation. The text (facing the mummy) reads, "Words spoken by the lector priest (and) *sem* priest: 'your purification is the purification of Horus, and vice versa; your purification is the purification of Seth, and vice versa; your purification is the purification of Thoth, and vice versa; your purification is the purification of Dunanwy, and vice versa.'"

2 "WORDS SPOKEN BY" *ḏd mdw in (djed medu in)* The strokes mean this could be "recitations." The sign *in* is the preposition "by."

2

3 "THE LECTOR PRIEST [AND] SEM PRIEST" *ẖry-ḥbt sm (khery-hebet sem)* In this case, rather than a name, the speaker has two titles. The first of these is *ẖry-ḥbt*, "lector priest," literally "he who is under the ritual book," from the preposition *ẖr*, "under" (but here meaning "carries"), and *ḥbt*, "ritual book." The second title is more usually written *sm*, "sem priest"—one who conducts such rituals and is often dressed in a leopard skin.

3

4 "YOUR PURIFICATION IS THE PURIFICATION OF HORUS AND VICE VERSA" *ʿbw·k ʿbw ḥr ṯz-pẖr (abuek abu her tjez-pekher)* The sign appears frequently in the formula and reads *ʿbw*, "purification." The first example has the suffix *·k*, and reads *ʿbw·k* "your purification"; this is followed by the same word with a direct genitive of the falcon (for the god *ḥr*, "Horus"), thus "the purification of Horus." This is a nonverbal sentence (see page 46), because the phrases are linked by an implicit form of the verb "to be"—"your purification is the purification of Horus." The signs and form an ancient phrase, *ṯz-pẖr*, which means, in effect, "vice versa"; in other words, "the purification of Horus is your purification." Some texts use all the words; others use this abbreviation.

4

5 "YOUR PURIFICATION IS THE PURIFICATION OF . . ." *ʿbw·k ʿbw . . . ṯz-pẖr (abuek abu . . . tjez-pekher)* The formula is repeated three more times, with a new god each time: Seth (*swty*), Thoth (*ḏḥwty*), and Dunanwy (*dwn-ʿnwy*)—the latter is a little-known deity that is associated with the eighteenth province of Upper Egypt. Seth (, the only god shown on the right) is written without a characteristic determinative; although he had to be named, his murder of Osiris made it inappropriate to have an image of him in the tomb in case it interfered magically with the burial and afterlife of the deceased.

5

THE STELA OF SAMONTU

It is thought that this Twelfth-Dynasty limestone stela may have come from Abydos in Upper Egypt, an ancient religious site and the cult center of Osiris. Many people were commemorated at Abydos, though after the Early Dynastic period no kings were buried there. The stela pays homage to a royal scribe called Samontu, whose name appears in the second column. There are three distinct parts of the stela: at the top is a biographical text; beneath this is a simple offering formula with a beautifully rendered scene of Samontu and his wife receiving offerings; and at the bottom there is a scene containing figures that include Samontu's three sons and two daughters. Samontu lived during the reigns of at least three kings of the Twelfth Dynasty.

1 "SCRIBE SAMONTU, LORD OF VENERATION" *zš zꜣ-mnṯw nb ỉmꜣḫ (zesh za-montju neb imakh)* The name of the commemorated, Samontu, is in the second column (after , "scribe," *zš*). The signs *mn* + *ṯ* + *w* for the god Montu are followed by the word *zꜣ*, "son." Unfortunately, there is no determinative to mark this clearly (and this is true for the rest of the text), but the next sign, *nb*, belongs to an epithet following the name. The second word of this is , which is a whole word-sign reading *ỉmꜣḫ*, referring to a state of veneration after death. So the person is "Samontu, lord of veneration."

2 "REGNAL YEAR THREE, UNDER THE MAJESTY OF THE KING OF UPPER AND LOWER EGYPT, NUBKAURE, GIVEN LIFE LIKE RE" *rnpt zp 3 ḫr ḥm n nswt-bỉty nwb-kꜣw-rꜥ dỉ ꜥnḫ mỉ rꜥ (renpet zep 3 kher hem en nesut-bity nub-kau-re di ankh mi re)* At the very top of the monument, the horizontal text provides the date of the stela. (The inclusion of dates on monuments is less common than

1
2
3
4

Egyptologists would like.) It can be seen (as explained on page 51) that the first signs are for "regnal year," followed by the number three, so this is "regnal year three." The long cartouche contains the name of the king, including a few extra words that are not usually part of the name but are sometimes written in cartouches. The first is , *ḥr*, a preposition usually meaning "with" or "near;" accompanying the name of a king, it is best translated as "under."

The next word is made up of the biliteral sign , which reads *ḥm* with a stroke after it—an example of a biliteral that is almost never written with phonetic complements. This refers to the "majesty" of the king and is usually followed, as it is here, by the genitive *n*. The next four signs comprise a very common group: read *nswt-bỉty*, which means "king of Upper and Lower Egypt"—the *nswt* is probably the original word for the Upper Egyptian king, and the *bỉty* his Lower Egyptian counterpart. Now we have the actual name *rꜥ* + *nwb* + *kꜣw*; when we transpose the *rꜥ* to the end, we have *nwb-kꜣw-rꜥ*, "Nubkaure" ("Golden are the Souls of Re"), which is the throne name for Amenemhat II. The final signs are epithets of the king, parts of which have already been seen separately (see page 53): *dỉ ꜥnḫ mỉ rꜥ*, "given life like Re."

3

3 "HE SAYS: 'I WAS BORN IN THE TIME OF THE MAJESTY OF THE KING OF UPPER AND LOWER EGYPT, SEHETEPIBRE, TRUE OF VOICE'" *ḏd·f ms·ỉ m rk ḥm n nswt-bỉty sḥtp-ỉb-rꜥ mꜣꜥ-ḫrw (djedef mesi em rek hem en nesut-bity sehetep-ib-re maa-kheru)* This text is too long for all of it to be deciphered here; however, after Samontu's name there is an interesting passage. The first word is *ḏd*, the verb "to speak"; it has a suffix *·f* and therefore means "he speaks" and introduces Samontu's words. (Because he is not a god or a king, he does not use *ḏd mdw*.) The biliteral *ms* has a phonetic complement *s*, to give the verb "to be born/give birth." It has the suffix , *·ỉ*, after it, so it means here "I was born." *m* is the common preposition "in," and + spell out a word *rk*, meaning "era" or "time." The next two groups are also in the long cartouche discussed on the facing page, and they are followed by the cartouche *sḥtp-ỉb-rʿ*, which is the throne name of Amenemhat I, the first king of the dynasty. The two long, flat signs following the cartouche are and , the most common abbreviation for *mꜣʿ-ḫrw*, "true of voice," meaning here that the king referred to is already dead (see page 73).

4 "'I WAS A YOUTH WHO TIED THE HEADBAND UNDER HIS MAJESTY, WHO PROCEEDED IN PEACE [IN THE TIME OF] THE KING OF UPPER AND LOWER EGYPT, KHEPERKARE, MAY HE LIVE FOREVER.'" *ỉnk ḥwn ṯz mḏḥ ḫr ḥm·f sḏꜣ m ḥtp [m rk] nswt-bỉty ḫpr-kꜣ-rʿ ʿnḫ ḏt (inek huen tjez medjeh kher hemef sedja em hetep [em rek] nesut-bity kheper-ka-re ankh djet)* The next word, , (see page 46) is a pronoun that means "I" and is one way in ancient Egyptian of marking a nonverbal sentence, "I am/I was"—but what was he? The hieroglyph could be one of several words for a young person, such as *ḥwn*, "youth," or *ẖrd* "child": "I was a youth." The two signs , *ṯz*, and , *mḏḥ*, both written without any phonetic complements or determinatives, are, respectively, the verb "to tie" (here it reads "who tied") and the noun "headband." Tying a headband seems to have been a rite of passage into manhood. This is followed by the preposition *ḫr* ("under," see page 92) and the noun *ḥm·f*, to give "under his majesty." The hieroglyphs at the top of the next column are + , *sḏꜣ*, meaning "who proceeds," with the preposition *m* and the word *ḥtp*, which has a few meanings, but with the preposition *m* usually means "in peace." You will see that the next hieroglyphs are the name of another king, so it seems that the scribe here did not bother to write words for "in the time of." The name of the king in the cartouche (in the fourth column from the right) is *ḫpr-kꜣ-rʿ*, "Kheperkare," Amenemhat I's son and successor, otherwise known as Senwosret I (see pages 80 to 81). The group of signs after the cartouche make up another common epithet of kings, made with the verb *ʿnḫ*, "to live," and the word *ḏt*, "eternity." The phrase is usually translated "may he live forever."

THE TOMB OF SENNEFER

Sennefer was the mayor of Thebes under Amenhotep II, in about 1420 BC. His West Bank tomb is elaborate and unusual for having a highly decorated burial chamber, in which the vibrant paintings still survive. Although the tomb is renowned for its ceiling of painted vines, the chamber is mostly decorated with scenes of Sennefer and his wife, Meryt, receiving offerings, as here. The accompanying formula reads (in part): "An offering which the king gives to Osiris, ruler of eternity, that he might give invocation offerings of bread, beer, oxen, and fowl, and all good and pure things that come forth upon his offering table in the course of every day."

1 "AN OFFERING WHICH THE KING GIVES" *ḥtp di͗ nswt (hetep di nesut)* This simple formula (see pages 53 to 55) opens with 𓇓 + 𓂞 + 𓊵, to read *ḥtp di͗ nswt*, "an offering which the king gives." Unlike the example given on page 53, 𓂞 has been written before 𓊵 to make the best use of the available space.

2 "OSIRIS, RULER OF ETERNITY" *wsir ḥqꜣ ḏt (usir heqa djet)* The name of those to whom offerings are made follows. The god is 𓁹 + 𓊨 + 𓀭, a variant writing of *wsi͗r*, "Osiris." The sign 𓋾 is a triliteral, *ḥqꜣ*, "ruler," and the *q* after it is the word's standard phonetic complement (of just the middle consonant, unusually). The following word is *ḏt*, "eternity." The epithet is "ruler of eternity."

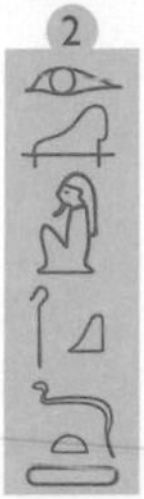

3 "THAT HE MIGHT GIVE INVOCATION OFFERINGS OF BREAD, BEER, OXEN, AND FOWL" *di͗·f prt-ḫrw t ḥnqt kꜣw ꜣpdw (dief peret-kheru te henqet kaw apedu)* The next part tells us about the offerings the god will give, and is introduced by *di͗·f*, "that he might give." The first group is *prt-ḫrw*, "invocation offerings," and the hieroglyphs for bread, beer, oxen, and fowl show what is being presented.

4 "AND ALL GOOD AND PURE THINGS" *ḫt nbt nfrt wꜥbt (khet nebet nefret wabet)* At the top of the next column is *ḫt*, "thing," followed by three adjectives, all taking the feminine form to agree with *ḫt*: *nbt*, *nfrt*, and a new sign, , *wꜥbt*, "pure."

5 "THAT COME FORTH UPON HIS OFFERING TABLE" *prrt nbt ḥr wdḥw·f (pereret nebet her wedhuef)* The next word, *prrt*, also agrees with *ḫt*, "thing" (see 4, above)—*prrt* comes from the verb *pr*, "to go forth," and it has its own adjective, *nbt*, agreeing with it. Therefore this means "everything that comes forth." The next word is the preposition *ḥr*, "upon," and of course we expect a noun to go with it, which is , a whole-word sign that reads *wdḥw* and means "offering table," used here with a third-person possessive, *·f*, to give "his offering table."

OFFERING FORMULAS AND TABLES

Offering formulas appear on almost every stela and tomb wall because the need for offerings in the afterlife was paramount to an Egyptian. Although this book contains only simple examples, many monuments bear very elaborate sets of wishes, and not just for the sorts of physical offerings mentioned in the tomb of Sennefer. An official of the Old Kingdom wanted the offering to ensure "that this his tomb may be given to him and that he may be buried in it"; other officials ask that particular offerings be made at various festivals, which tell us something about the main events that were celebrated by the ancient Egyptians.

Offering tables themselves came in a variety of forms. They were often made of stone and placed before a divine shrine or tomb stela, and the needs of the god or the deceased were placed on them, where they could be magically consumed by that deity or the person's spirit. Offering tables are depicted in temples and tombs, often groaning with the wonderful array of produce being presented on them.

6 "IN THE COURSE OF EVERY DAY" *m ẖrt-hrw nt rꜥ nb (em kheret-heru net re neb)* is an alternative for the very common , *m*, "in." is a highly abbreviated writing of the word *ẖrt-hrw*, "duration, course [of time]," and the *nt* following this is the feminine genitive "of" (see page 44). The text ends with *rꜥ nb*, "every day," and so texts 3 to 6 refer to how offerings made to the gods were then redistributed to temple employees and favored individuals.

7 "FOR THE *KA* SPIRIT OF THE MAYOR OF THE SOUTHERN CITY, SENNEFER, JUSTIFIED" *n kꜣ n hꜣty-ꜥ n niwt rsy(t) sn-nfr mꜣꜥ-ẖrw (en ka en haty-a en niut resey(t) sen-nefer maa-kheru)* The person to whom the offering is made comes next—*n kꜣ n*, "for the *ka*-spirit of." The deceased's *ka*-spirit lives in the tomb and is sustained by the offerings made there. There follows the title *hꜣty-ꜥ n niwt rsy(t)*, "mayor of the southern city [Thebes]," and the name, *sn-nfr*, "Sennefer," plus the obligatory term "justified," or "true of voice," given to the dead who have passed judgment.

8 "HIS SISTER, HIS BELOVED, THE SINGER OF AMUN, MERYT, JUSTIFIED" *snt·f mr(t)·f šmꜥyt n imn mryt mꜣꜥt-ẖrw (senetef meretef shemayet en amun meryt maat-kheru)* The first word is *snt* with the suffix *·f*, "his sister." In the New Kingdom, this usage does not indicate brother–sister marriage; "sister" is a synonym for "wife." The following sign, , has the phonetic value *mr* and is a compact way to write the verb "to love." Here it is used as a noun with the possessive suffix *·f*, meaning "his beloved." The feminine seems to have been omitted or a | stroke was used instead. The next words are her title: you will recognize the name of the god Amun, ; the sign has the value *šmꜥ*, and with the small before it this word reads *šmꜥyt*, "singer," and so she is a "singer of Amun." The next four signs are followed by the female determinative , and so her name is *mryt*. Lastly, you see the feminine version of the word for "justified"—note the extra *t*, reading *mꜣꜥt-ẖrw*.

THE TOMB OF NEFERTARI

This detail of text from the tomb of Nefertari, wife of Ramesses II, in the Valley of the Queens, is useful because it combines some phrase-types that have already been encountered. (Nefertari's cartouche can be seen above and to the right of the figure in this scene.)

The selected passage (on the right face of the pillar shown here) reads, "Words spoken by Horus, who avenges his father: 'I am your son, your beloved, who came forth from your limbs.'" Once the visitor has deciphered the beginning of the text, it is easier to understand exactly how it relates to the scene on the adjacent face of the pillar. On that face is a mummiform figure in a white robe (visible left), wearing the white crown of Upper Egypt. This is the classic manner of showing Osiris, god of the dead and father of Horus, and if you look closely at the face's first column you will see that it begins with , one of the two main ways of writing the god's name.

1 "WORDS SPOKEN BY HORUS, WHO AVENGES HIS FATHER" *ḏd mdw i͗n ḥr nḏ ḥr i͗t·f (djed medu in her nedj her itef)* The column begins with this well-known formula (see page 52). The next sign is a falcon, which is the usual writing of Horus (*ḥr*), but several more signs add to the name. The first is , the biliteral *nḏ* ("to avenge"), which is almost always, and inexplicably, complemented by the sign , and the determinative. They are followed by the preposition *ḥr*, which indirectly introduces who is being avenged. The signs that write the words *i͗t* + *·f* = *i͗t·f*, "his father," may be familiar from page 83; here they are again, this time written more helpfully with in front. This form of Horus is common, being a reference to the time after Osiris's death when Horus fought Seth to avenge his father's murder; as in this illustration, this form of Horus is usually shown as a priest rather than a hawk-headed man.

2 "'I AM YOUR SON, YOUR BELOVED, WHO CAME FORTH FROM YOUR LIMBS'" *i͗nk zꜣ·k mry·k pr m ḥꜥw·k (inek zaek meryek per em hawek)* The next text describes what Horus is saying. You may recognize the signs for *i͗nk*, a pronoun for "I," which introduces one of the nonverbal sentences, "I am" (see page 46). Then *zꜣ·k* is "your son" and *mry·k* is "your beloved," a noun made from the verb *mr* (which can be written with either the hoe sign or the channel sign —both read *mr*). The verb *pr*, "to come forth," should also be familiar, and the next three signs form another phrase, "who comes forth," which gives further information about the son. *m* used here means "from," while the noun *ḥꜥ* means "flesh, limb." Here is an old-fashioned plural with the triple repetition of the determinative, and the addition of a second-person suffix, thus *ḥꜥw·k* "your limbs." Horus, avenger of his father, is saying, "I am your son, your beloved, who came forth from your limbs."

THE STELA OF HETEP

Egyptian commemorative tablets, known as stelae (see page 24), generally take two forms. The first is rectangular and is composed of several jambs and architraves; it serves rather like a door, through which the dead person's soul can move between this world and the next. (Egyptologists refer to these as "false doors.") The second type of stela is also rectangular in shape but has a rounded top. The Twelfth-Dynasty stela of Hetep (shown left, provenance unknown) is a classic example of this kind. This style is more common than the other type of stelae and can range from massive royal monuments in stone to small wooden tablets. The inscription here (left) begins with a *hetep di nesut* formula (see pages 53 to 55). The dedication naming Hetep is at the end (3), before the names of what are believed to be his father and grandfather at the bottom.

1 "OSIRIS, LORD OF DJEDU" *wsir nb ḏdw (usir neb djedu)* The first two signs shown on the right give the name "Osiris." (On the stela itself they follow the offering formula that is explained in detail on pages 53 to 55). His epithet here is , *nb ḏdw*, "lord of Djedu." , *ḏd*, is a common biliteral, and frequently has the phonetic complement . Because it is a place—the Delta town of Busiris, where Osiris's cult may have originated before it became principally concentrated at Abydos—it has the sign ⊗, the determinative of a town. The of the name is, unusually, written after the determinative, probably to best fit the space.

2 "THE GREAT GOD, LORD OF ABYDOS" *nṯr ꜥꜣ nb ꜣbḏw (netjer aa neb abdju)* The epithet *nṯr ꜥꜣ*, "the great god," has been seen before (see page 67). It is followed by another epithet, the first word of which is *nb*, either "all" or "lord," depending on the context. In this case we deduce that *nb* means "lord" because of the place-name (recognizable by the ⊗ determinative) that comes straight after. So the location is . The sign has two possible phonetic values: *ꜣb* and *mr*. By looking at adjacent signs, we pick up clues as to which it is: the most common value of is *ḏw*, which would give either *ꜣbḏw* or *mrḏw*. If you go to the vocabulary list, you will find only one, *ꜣbḏw*, which is the Egyptian name for Abydos. Thus the text reads, "lord of Abydos."

3 "FOR THE HONORED ONE, THE STEWARD HETEP" *n imꜣḫw imy r pr ḥtp (en imakhu imy-re per hetep)* The offerings specified (left, and explained in detail on pages 53 to 55) are followed by the dedication (right) to the person for whom the offerings are intended: the dative *n* is followed by the word *imꜣḫw*. A person who is *imꜣḫw* is one who is honored or venerated (in origin, it meant one for whom all had been provided). This is followed by the title *imy-r pr*, "steward," and the name *ḥtp*, "Hetep," without a determinative, to give, "the honored one, the steward Hetep."

A LION HUNT SCARAB OF AMENHOTEP III

Amenhotep III (r. 1390–1352 BC) was one of a select few Egyptian kings who produced a number of "scarabs" (so called because the reverse side is fashioned in the form of a scarab beetle), bearing texts commemorating events such as animal hunts, a marriage, and the creation of a lake, among other things. More than two hundred of these scarabs have survived. It is not known exactly why they were made, though they may have been given to officials as a mark of royal favor. The scarab shown here is one of a pair that was issued by Amenhotep III in the tenth year of his reign. The royal titles that are given in the middle area (which are sometimes indistinct as they were incised into a mold) are examined on the facing page. This particular example is a "lion hunt scarab," its name derived from the accomplishments noted in the text. The signs indicate that the king himself shot 102 lions with his bow over a period of ten years.

1 "KING OF UPPER AND LOWER EGYPT, LORD OF APPEARANCES" *nswt-bity nb ḫꜥw (nesut-bity neb khau)* The main part of the royal name begins with the expression, "king of Upper and Lower Egypt." It is followed by, *nb*, "lord." The next sign () is for *ḫꜥ*, which can mean either "to appear" or "appearance." Coming after *nb* it is a noun, and it is plural, *ḫꜥw*, so the epithet is "lord of appearances." Referring to the ways in which a king could manifest himself to his subjects, in royal and semidivine roles, this is a distinctly Egyptian use of the word "appearance."

2 "NEBMAATRE, SON OF RE" *nb-mꜣꜥt-rꜥ zꜣ rꜥ (neb-maat-re za re)* In line four, two cartouches are separated by the signs for "son of Re." The first cartouche, *nb-mꜣꜥt-rꜥ*, "Nebmaatre," was on the earlier king list (see page 63), but there is an interesting difference in the order of the second and third signs: + is here +. This again reveals the flexibility of hieroglyphic writing—the ordering is almost certainly due to the neater arrangement of under.

3 "AMENHOTEP, RULER OF THEBES, GIVEN LIFE AND DOMINION" *ỉmn-ḥtp ḥqꜣ wꜣst dỉ ꜥnḫ wꜣs (Amen-hotep heqa waset di ankh was)* The next cartouche has four signs that give *ỉmn-ḥtp*, "Amenhotep." Two further signs form a descriptive epithet: , *ḥqꜣ*, "ruler," and , the name of Thebes, *wꜣst*—so he is "ruler of Thebes." The last three hieroglyphs denote attributes "given" (), *dỉ*, to him: *ꜥnḫ* and *wꜣs*, "life and dominion."

4 "GREAT WIFE OF THE KING, TIYE, MAY SHE LIVE FOREVER" *ḥmt nswt wrt tỉyỉ ꜥnḫ·tỉ ḏt (hemet nesut weret tiyi ankhti djet)* In the next line, the phrase *ḥmt nswt wrt*, "great wife of the king," may be familiar (see page 67). It indicates that the cartouche is the name of a queen. It reads + + + , *tỉ + y + ỉ + ỉ*, to give, *tỉyỉ*. Amenhotep III's principal wife was Queen Tiye. Her epithets are *ꜥnḫ* (the verb "to live") and *ḏt* ("forever"); the ending, , *tỉ*, means the verb is expressing a wish for a female, thus "may she live forever."

A LINTEL OF AMENEMHAT III

This lintel consists of a central column, either side of which are four symmetrical columns. The texts provide compelling evidence that the lintel originated in the Faiyum, which was famed for its natural lake (see page 106). Amenemhat III (r. 1831–1786 BC) played an important role in helping to develop this part of the country. He constructed two pyramids, one near the Faiyum at Hawara. The inscription on the lintel shown here reads, "king of Upper and Lower Egypt, lord of the Two Lands, Nimaatre, beloved of Sebek of Shedyt. Words spoken: 'I have given to you all life and dominion like Re; beloved of Horus, who dwells in Shedyt, lord of the Faiyum; son of Re, his beloved, Amenemhat.'"

1 "KING OF UPPER AND LOWER EGYPT, LORD OF THE TWO LANDS, NIMAATRE" *nswt bity nb tꜣwy n-mꜣꜥt-rꜥ (nesut bity neb tawy ni-maat-re)* The central column of the lintel begins with "king of Upper and Lower Egypt, lord of the Two Lands," followed by a cartouche written *rꜥ + n + mꜣꜥt*, read *n-mꜣꜥt-rꜥ*, "Nimaatre," the praenomen of Amenemhat III of the Twelfth Dynasty.

2 "BELOVED OF SEBEK OF SHEDYT" *mry sbk šdyt (mery sebek shedyt)* The next column (moving out from the center and right), is simpler than it looks. At the bottom are the hieroglyphs for *mry*, "beloved of," which usually follows the name of a god. Here it is the crocodile god with the plumes at the top. Its name is spelled out in single hieroglyphs behind the plumes: *sbk*, "Sebek." This deity is particularly associated with the Faiyum depression to the west of the Nile (see page 106). The sign used in the lintel is not in the regular sign list (hence it is illustrated more conventionally here, right), with the determinative for the name of Sebek being an elaborate variant of , wearing a crown and holding a scepter with an additional pair of arms. But note there are two very odd signs below the arms protruding from the crocodile and holding a scepter. Again, this sign is not one that is in the regular sign list, although it is probably based on the shrine-sign  with an animal head protruding. It is an occasional writing of the place-name *šdyt*, "Shedyt," which the Greeks called Crocodilopolis (modern-day Medinet el-Fayum), more simply written , using the biliteral , *šd*. Shedyt was the cult center of Sebek.

3 "WORDS SPOKEN" *ḏd mdw (djed medu)* This formula should now be easily recognized (see page 52).

4 "'I HAVE GIVEN TO YOU ALL LIFE AND DOMINION LIKE RE'" *dı͗·n·(ı͗) n·k ꜥnḫ wꜣs nb mı͗ rꜥ (dieni enek ankh was neb mi re)* This is similar to the earlier temple inscription of Senwosret III (see page 86), with *dı͗·n·(ı͗) n·k* translating as "I have given to you" and

SEBEK AND THE FAIYUM

Several references on the Amenemhat III temple lintel suggest the Faiyum as the lintel's place of origin (see page 104). A large fertile depression to the west of the Nile Valley, the Faiyum received most of its water via a channel of the Nile that branched off north of Asyut. Although inhabited in prehistoric times, the area was probably not much developed until the Middle Kingdom, when Amenemhat III appears to have taken a particular interest in it. One of his most important initiatives was to increase cultivable land in the area through irrigation and other projects.

The Faiyum was one of the main cult centers of the crocodile god Sebek. The center was at *šdyt* (Shedyt, Greek Crocodilopolis, modern Medinet el-Fayum), and it is clear that a form of Horus was also worshipped there. Ancient Egyptians considered some crocodiles to be sacred and mummified them after death. Wherever crocodile deities are discovered in Egypt, it is assumed that the real-life creatures would have been found in the vicinity.

ʿnḫ wȝs nb "all life and dominion." The final two elements are *mi rʿ*—"like Re."

5

5 "'BELOVED OF HORUS WHO DWELLS IN SHEDYT, LORD OF THE FAIYUM'" *mry ḥr ḥr-ib šdyt nb tȝ-š (mery her her-ib shedyt neb ta-she)* The following column faces the opposite direction from the rest of the text; again, at the bottom (see page 105) are the hieroglyphs for *mry*, "beloved of," , so we have the name of another god. At the top is a falcon, for which Horus (*ḥr*) is the most commonly associated deity. The name is further qualified by signs + that form a two-word compound preposition, *ḥr-ib*, which is literally, "on the heart of," but when used with gods tends to mean "where they dwell." The adjacent sign is *šdyt*, the place-name "Shedyt" (see 2 about the unusual sign, here replaced with). Thus the text reads "who dwells in Shedyt." The *nb* sign that follows suggests another place-name, a place of which he is "lord," and it is . The first sign, , is a common variant of without the grains of sand beneath, and it reads *tȝ*; the second sign is the pool hieroglyph *š*, and the third the determinative , which usually indicates a foreign or desert country. The name is read *tȝ-š*, and is one of the ancient names for the Faiyum. The use of the determinative for the Faiyum is revealing; although we think now of this region as part of Egypt, here it is treated as a land that is out on the periphery. Amenemhat III did much to integrate the area, whereupon it was written with the ⊗ determinative.

6

6 "SON OF RE, HIS BELOVED, AMENEMHAT" *zȝ rʿ mr·f imn-m-ḥȝt (za re meref amen-em-hat)* The last column gives another cartouche, but above it is *zȝ rʿ*, "son of Re" (see page 72), and the hieroglyph , discussed earlier (see page 52) as a less common spelling for words associated with the verb *mr*, "to love," which are shown elsewhere with the hoes or ; the stroke | shows that is being used as a noun. It is followed by the suffix *·f* and means "his beloved." The first three signs in the cartouche are the name of the god Amun, followed by *m* + *ḥȝ* + *t*, giving *imn-m-ḥȝt*, "Amenemhat."

UNITING THE TWO LANDS

As early as the First Dynasty, the common symbols of Egyptian unification were already developed. It was the religious duty of the king to keep the "Two Lands" of Upper and Lower Egypt together as one state. These separate but joined entities were maintained in a variety of ways—by means of crowns, protective deities, and

distinctive plants, among other things. The hieroglyph depicts the Red Crown of Lower Egypt, depicts the White Crown of Upper Egypt, and the combined crowns; shows the protective cobra Wadjet of Lower Egypt and the vulture Nekhbet of Upper Egypt. These last two signs are seen in the "Two Ladies," or *nebty*, name for the king (; see page 38). depicts the papyrus plant of Lower Egypt and depicts the sedge plant of Upper Egypt. A common visual expression of the union was to show the two plants twisted together around the hieroglyph , *zmꜣ*, a verb for "to unite." This process was referred to as "uniting of the Two Lands," *zmꜣ-tꜣwy*, and is frequently shown being carried out by two corpulent deities—as here, on the side of a colossal statue of the Twelfth-Dynasty ruler Senwosret I (though the texts actually date from the reign of King Merenptah in the Nineteenth Dynasty).

1

2

---

1 "WORDS SPOKEN" *ḏd mdw (djed medu)* Although this well-known "Words Spoken" formula is repeated at the top of each of these three columns, to indicate that the words below are spoken by the deities, the words should only be read once at the beginning of each text.

---

2 "'I HAVE GIVEN TO YOU ALL LIFE, STABILITY, AND DOMINION, ALL HEALTH, ALL JOY, LIKE RE FOREVER'" *dỉ·n·(ỉ) n·k ꜥnḫ ḏd wꜣs nb snb nb ꜣwt-ỉb nb mỉ rꜥ ḏt (dieni enek ankh djed was neb seneb neb aut-ib neb mi re djet)* The now-familiar construction *dỉ·n·(ỉ) n·k*, for "I have given to you" (see pages 86 and 105), is followed by the nouns *wꜣs* ("dominion"), *snb* ("health"), and *ꜣwt-ỉb* ("joy"), each qualified by the adjective *nb*, "all." The only word that is different in this phrase from those found in previous inscriptions is , *ḏd*, meaning "stability." The final elements are *mỉ rꜥ ḏt*—"like Re forever."

STATUE OF AMENWAHSU

This beautiful small statue of Amenwahsu, a high priest, possibly comes from the temple of Amun at Karnak in Thebes, and dates approximately to the reign of Thutmose III (r. 1479–1425 BC) of the Eighteenth Dynasty. Amenwahsu probably erected the monument to display his devotion to Re-Horakhty, Amun, and Montu, the gods named on it. The quartzite statue shows Amenwahsu presenting an inscribed stela (by implication to these same deities), and is designed to demonstrate his piety and the fact that he had access to sufficient wealth and power to pay for the creation of such a statue.

The inscription to the named gods that is shown on the statue is a form of worship or prayer. The section selected here translates as "Amun-Re-Horakhty, great god, lord of heaven; lord of heaven, ruler of Thebes. Adoring Re-Horakhty when he rises in the eastern horizon of the sky, by the high priest of Montu, lord of Thebes [and] lord of Tod, Amenwahsu, true of voice in peace."

1 "AMUN-RE-HORAKHTY, GREAT GOD, LORD OF HEAVEN"
ỉmn-rʿ-ḥr-ꜣḫty nṯr ʿꜣ nb pt (amen-re-her-akhty netjer aa neb pet)
At the top of the statue is a ram-headed god in a boat with a sun disc on his head. The god's name is to the right of the figure. The first signs compose the name of Amun, but there is another name below, . The sign list shows that  is mostly used in the name of the god Re-Horakhty; it combines *rʿ* + *ḥr* and is followed by two signs reading *ꜣḫty* (see page 77). The god's name can therefore be read *rʿ-ḥr-ꜣḫty*. The name of Amun at the beginning indicates this is a composite of both these deities, which would be translated as "Amun-Re-Horakhty." Below this are hieroglyphs  +  that read *nṯr ʿꜣ*, "great god," and *nb pt*, "lord of heaven."

2 "LORD OF HEAVEN, RULER OF THEBES" *nb pt ḥqꜣ wꜣst (neb pet heqa waset)* To the left of the god is a more abbreviated *nb pt* (see above, "lord of heaven"), as well as *ḥqꜣ wꜣst*, "ruler of Thebes."

3 "ADORING RE-HORAKHTY WHEN HE RISES IN THE EASTERN HORIZON OF THE SKY" *dwꜣ rʿ-ḥr-ꜣḫty ḫft wbn·f m ꜣḫt ỉꜣbt nt pt (dua re-her-akhty khefet webenef em akhet iabet net pet)* Below the god, the first two lines present a brief hymn to the god. The first sign, , can have a couple of possible readings, but  suggests that it is *dwꜣ*, because it is a determinative for words indicating worship; *dwꜣ* is a verb meaning "to adore" and here it functions as an opening caption (see page 47) meaning "adoring." The object is Re-Horakhty (explained above). Then there are three single-sound signs: *ḫ* + *f* + *t*, *ḫft*—this can be a preposition "in front of," but when followed by a verb it often means "when." The next four signs, three single-character hieroglyphs, *w* + *b* + *n*, and the determinative , form the verb *wbn*, "to rise"; they are followed by the suffix pronoun *·f*. So *ḫft wbn·f* means "when he rises." Something to do with the sky, or similar, might be anticipated next.  is the preposition *m*; the noun *ꜣḫt* is "horizon"; the following word is *ỉꜣbt*, "east"; then comes *nt* (feminine genitive), agreeing with *ꜣḫt* and *pt*, "sky": "Adoring

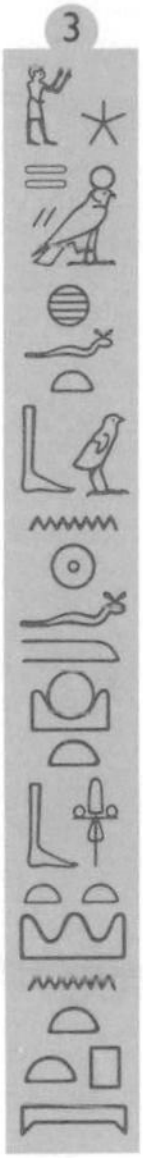

A POWERFUL PRIESTHOOD

The statue of Amenwahsu (see page 110) mentions the god Montu as both the lord of Thebes and the lord of Tod, and Amenwahsu may have been a priest in both of these places. From about the Middle Kingdom onward many high officials commissioned statues of themselves and placed them in temples to demonstrate their owners' importance, wealth, and devotion. The number of gods mentioned in Amenwahsu's text is high, an expression of his allegiance to several major state deities as well as to the one for whom he served as a priest.

The statue bears a carving of Amun-Re-Horakhty, shown in a boat or barque. Seen in many tombs in the Valley of the Kings, this is a common depiction of solar deities, who were thought to travel across the sky, and through the underworld, in this familiar form of Egyptian transport. The divine images of the gods were also moved from one temple to another in large model boats, carried on the shoulders of faithful priests.

Re-Horakhty when he rises in the eastern horizon of the sky." This very simple text describes what Amenwahsu is doing, and is one of the standard ways to begin a hymn.

4 "BY THE HIGH PRIEST OF MONTU, LORD OF THEBES" *in ḥm-nṯr tpy n mnṯw nb wꜣst (in hem-netjer tepy en montu neb waset)* The rest of the text consists of a title and a name, introduced by the preposition *in*, "by." The first three signs are . Although *ḥm* was seen earlier as "majesty," it can also, and more often, mean "servant"; so what is written here is *ḥm-nṯr*, "servant of god," or "priest," a common title. The sign list shows that the dagger reads *tpy*, "first," so the full title is "first priest" or "high priest." Such titles are usually followed by the name of the relevant god; in this case the deity is *mnṯw nb wꜣst*, "Montu, lord of Thebes." Note that the *w* of *mnṯw* is written with rather than .

5 "THE HIGH PRIEST OF MONTU, LORD OF TOD, AMENWAHSU, TRUE OF VOICE IN PEACE" *ḥm-ntr tpy n mnṯw nb ḏrty imn-wꜣḥ-sw mꜣꜥ-ḫrw m ḥtp (hem-netjer tepy en montu neb djerty amen-wah-su maa-kheru em hetep)* The first signs repeat *ḥm-nṯr tpy n mnṯw*, "high priest of Montu," given earlier (4, above). Following this, the place-name reads *ḏrty*, the name of Tod, a town south of Thebes. The name Amenwahsu takes up much of the last line, . The name of Amun may be familiar by now, but the sign has not been seen before and can be read either *sk* or *wꜣḥ*. has been seen but mostly as an abbreviation for *nswt*, "king." Here it has the normal phonetic value *sw*; if it meant "king" it would probably be given at the beginning of the name. So how do we read ? Unfortunately, only experience can help here. Other examples tell us the sign should read *wꜣḥ*, so we get *imn-wꜣḥ-sw*, Amenwahsu. The sign is the standard New Kingdom determinative for a deceased or noble person. The last four signs are an extension of the "true of voice" epithet (see page 73), using the preposition *m* and *ḥtp*, "peace" (not "offering").

JUDGMENT OF HUNEFER

This papyrus, which dates to the beginning of the Nineteenth Dynasty (ca. 1275 BC), shows a detail from an illustration in the Book of the Dead that belonged to Hunefer, a royal scribe. The whole sequence shows Hunefer being brought into the presence of Osiris by Anubis and Horus. The scene is confirmed as a judgment of the dead because a feather, representing *maat* (a complex sense of ethics that tied personal behavior to the maintenance of cosmic order), is weighed against a pot, which symbolizes Hunefer's heart.

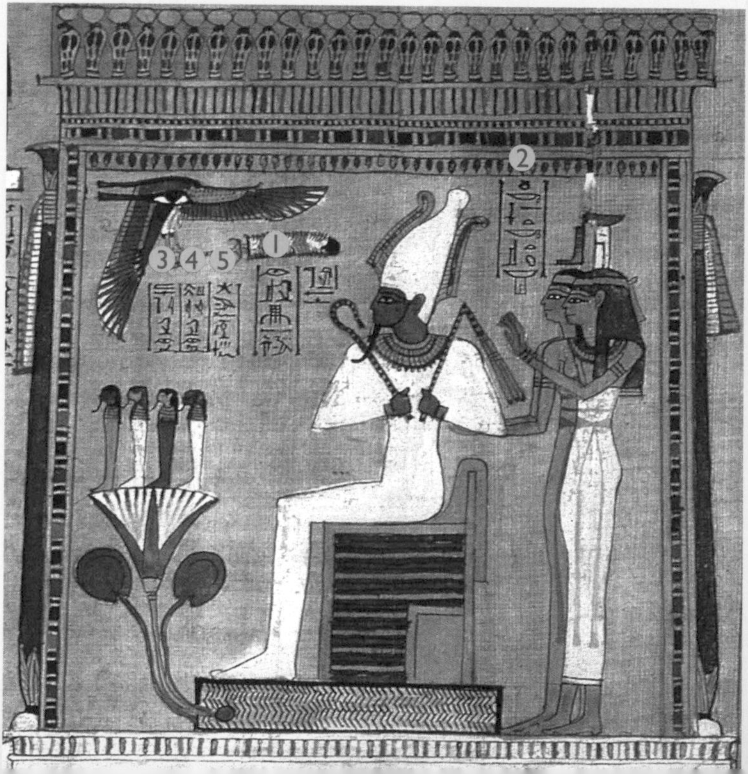

Osiris, wearing the white crown, is shown at the center of this detail from the papyrus. He is seated under a canopy, accompanied by two women. Under the canopy are the names of several gods; the hieroglyphs are written with a brush on papyrus, and are therefore not as clear as the carved and painted signs that have been discussed on the preceding pages.

1 "OSIRIS, FOREMOST OF THE WESTERNERS, THE GREAT GOD" *wsỉr ḫnty-ỉmntyw nṯr ꜥꜣ (usir khenty-imentyu netjer aa)* Osiris's names and epithets are written in the two columns in front of his crook. After his name is , *ḫnty imntyw*, "foremost of the Westerners," written out here to include the bird , *tyw*. The short second column holds *nṯr ꜥꜣ*, "the great god." Note that the word *nṯr* has a determinative , which it does not always have when used elsewhere (for example, see page 111).

2 "I AM YOUR SISTER ISIS, I AM YOUR SISTER NEPHTHYS" *ỉnk snt·k ꜣst ỉnk snt·k nbt-ḥwt (inek senetek ast, inek senetek nebet-hut)* Behind Osiris stand two women with hieroglyphs on their heads, and ; is part of the name of the goddess Isis, while is made up of , *nb*, and , *ḥwt*, and is the Egyptian form of the Greek name Nephthys, *nbt-ḥwt*. These deities were sisters of Osiris. There is more text above their raised hands. We have seen the pronoun "I," *ỉnk*, used several times in the nonverbal construction "I am." The next word has a *·k* suffix, and consists of the biliteral sign with phonetic complement and a feminine *t* ending. The word *snt* means "sister," which fits the context here. The last two hieroglyphs repeat the two divine names shown on the heads of the goddesses; we should read *ỉnk snt·k* once for each goddess.

3 "IMSETY" *ỉmsty (imsety)* In front of Osiris is a lily bearing four small mummiform figures. (Although often referred to as a lotus, the plant that actually existed in ancient Egypt was *Nymphaea*

SPELLS FOR THE DEAD

The best-known Egyptian funerary text is the Book of the Dead, which consisted of a series of spells and instructions written on a papyrus to enable the deceased to negotiate his or her way past various obstacles in the underworld, or Duat, and into the afterlife. From the early New Kingdom onward, it became the custom to bury such a book with the deceased—or, at least, with those who could afford to commission one. These texts contained certain typical elements and common motifs, including a process of final judgment observed by Osiris, attended by his sisters Isis and Nephthys. The dead person is protected by the so-called four sons of Horus, who are often shown on the canopic jars, which contain the embalmed internal organs. The Egyptians believed that the heart was the seat of intelligence, and that it kept a record of a person's good and bad deeds. If the deceased was judged worthy, he or she was free to pass into the presence of Osiris. If not, the fearsome Ammut, a hybrid of lion, hippopotamus, and crocodile, lay in wait to administer divine retribution by devouring the heart and denying eternal life to the deceased.

caerulea, a blue water lily.) Due to lack of space, the names for these four figures are squashed into three columns above them. For some unknown reason, the first two columns have the name of Osiris at the bottom; note that the hieroglyphs immediately above both examples of end with the divine determinative . Unfortunately, the space problem meant that the scribe could not put such determinatives into the final column, which contains two names. The signs for the first column are: *m* + *z* + *tỉ* + *ỉ*, *mzty*, which can also be written *ỉmsty*, "Imsety." It is the name of one of the protective deities often depicted on the canopic jars containing the embalmed internal organs of many ancient Egyptians; these gods are known collectively as the "four sons of Horus". The lid of the canopic jar of Imsety usually took the form of a human head.

4

4 "HAPY" *ḥpy (hapy)* In the next column, is most often read *ḥp*, with the phonetic complement *p* here, and *y*, to give *ḥpy*, "Hapy," a son of Horus whose canopic jar lid is usually shown with the head of a baboon. With two of the sons of Horus named, the remaining two must be in the last column .

5

5 "DUAMUTEF [AND] QEBEHSENUEF" *dwꜣ-mwt·f qbḥ-snw·f (dua-mutef qebeh-senuef)* With the exception of , *qbḥ*, all the hieroglyphs in this column have been seen recently. The first name consists of , *dwꜣ*, "adore," and , *mwt*, "mother"—Duamutef, whose canopic jar lid is usually shown with the head of a jackal. The last name begins with , *qbḥ*, followed by the two-barbed arrowhead , *sn*, and *w*, with plural strokes, hence *snw*, to name Qebehsenuef, whose canopic jar lid is usually shown with the head of a falcon. (Readable elsewhere—in the fourth column of the papyrus text, not visible here—is the name of Hunefer accompanied by the word "Osiris," thus "the Osiris Hunefer," which was a standard way of referring to a person who has died and passed successfully through the judgment.)

THE RED CHAPEL OF HATSHEPSUT

PLANTS
Many signs were based on plants. The words for "countryside" and "peasant" include stylized flowering reeds, which reflect the lush vegetation of ancient Egypt's swampy land.

This block of quartzite comes from the red chapel of Queen Hatshepsut at Karnak, which was dismantled to make way for other buildings after her death. She was officially the regent of Thutmose III (who was the son of her husband, Thutmose II, by another wife),

but she seems to have assumed the kingship about seven years into his reign (ca. 1473 BC), although never denying the fact that he was king too, until her death in the twenty-second year of his reign. Much of the extensive building work she undertook was later damaged deliberately during a campaign of persecution of her memory carried out by Thutmose III in his sole reign. Many of her cartouches were spoiled at that time, whereas this block is perfectly preserved.

---

1 "PERFECT GOD, LORD OF CULT ACTION" *nṯr nfr nb ỉr ḫt (netjer nefer neb ir khet)* Beginning at the top right is a group of hieroglyphs for the expression *nṯr nfr nb ỉr ḫt*, meaning "perfect god, lord of cult action," followed by the queen's name. The small gap before the below shows that it belongs to a separate section of text.

---

2 "MAATKARE, GIVEN LIFE, STABILITY, DOMINION, AND HEALTH, LIKE RE, FOREVER" *mꜣꜥt-kꜣ-rꜥ dỉ ꜥnḫ ḏd wꜣs snb mỉ rꜥ ḏt (maat-ka-re di ankh djed was seneb mi re djet)* The signs in the cartouche should be familiar: *rꜥ* + the figure of the goddess *mꜣꜥt* + *kꜣ*, to give *mꜣꜥt-kꜣ-rꜥ*, "Maatkare," the queen's throne name. Then the hieroglyph *dỉ* is followed by a number of things given to her: *ꜥnḫ*, *ḏd*, *wꜣs*, and *snb*—life, stability, dominion, and health, respectively. The last two elements, *mỉ rꜥ* and *ḏt*, together read "like Re, forever."

---

3 "GIVING LAND FOUR TIMES" *wd sḫt zp 4 (wed sekhet zep 4)* The queen is undertaking two separate but linked rituals. The first is written vertically before the queen, . The reads *wd*, despite consisting of just the one sign, and is one of the normal writings of the verb , *wdỉ*, which has a variety of meanings, including "to give," "to put," and "to present." The next sign, , reads *sḫt*, and means "fields" or "area of land." The lack of internal detail in the signs of this text means that the next round sign looks like those read previously as , , or ; a clue as to which

of the three this is can be found in the four vertical strokes that follow. These write the number four (see page 50), and are often found with , *zp*, "time," or "occasion," so this means "four times."

4

4 "THE RUNNING OF THE APIS" *pḥrr ḥpw (peherer hepu)* The second ritual is , written horizontally at the bottom above the bull. The verb *pḥrr* means "to run" (note the determinative), and the noun *ḥpw* is the name of the bull, which appears below. The image acts effectively as a determinative to *ḥpw*. This is the Apis, the sacred bull of Memphis. So the ritual is "the running of the Apis," an ancient rite in Egypt that was associated with the periodic need to rejuvenate the king. The ancient Egyptian festival for the rejuvenation of the monarch was the Sed, and the two acts shown in this scene are core aspects of it.

5

5 "WORDS SPOKEN, 'WELCOME TO ME, WELCOME TO ME, IN PEACE, MY DAUGHTER, MY BELOVED'" *ḏd mdw iy·w(y) n·(i) zp 2 m ḥtp zꜣt·(i) mrt·(i) (djed medu iyeni zep 2 em hetep zati mereti)*
The other texts are in the two self-contained columns facing right, and are being spoken by a god, probably Amun, watching over the ceremony (to the left). This text is spoken in the first person, but there are no examples of the first person *i* suffix as , , and so on—rather like the *di·n·(i)* formula (see page 86), we have to add it. This practice is not unusual in formal texts, and it might imply that the ending was barely, if at all, pronounced. The first word is , which is derived from the verb *iy*, "to come." This is a special use in such contexts and expresses a greeting, read *iy·w(y)*, that translates as "Welcome!" Of the signs that follow, *n* has to be expanded to *n·(i)*, "to me," and the two strokes after the round sign write the number two, and so the sign is again , *zp*, "time" or "occasion," and therefore means "twice" or even "repeat." Earlier (see page 113) *m ḥtp* was shown to mean "in peace"; the whole greeting is therefore "Welcome to me, welcome to me, in peace." It is followed by the words *zꜣt* ("daughter") and *mrt*, which is either an adjective agreeing

with the feminine noun *zꜣt* or a noun meaning "beloved one." If we continue adding *·(i)* to these, we get "my daughter, my beloved" or "my beloved daughter." Note the consistency of gender.

6

6 "HATSHEPSUT, JOINED WITH AMUN, OF MY BODY" *ḥꜣt-špst ḫnm-ỉmn nt ẖt·(i) (hat-shepset khenem-amun net kheti)* The cartouche contains both the personal name of Hatshepsut and an epithet. As the first three signs write the name of Amun, the name is doubtless transposed. Try to identify the queen's name first:  reads *ḥꜣt*, and  functions here as a word sign and abbreviation for the word *šps*, with a *t* ending; *ḥꜣt-špst*, "Hatshepsut" (it is sometimes written as a plural *ḥꜣt-špswt*). So the other sign, , must go with *ỉmn* (the first three signs shown on the right); it indicates the verb *ḫnm*, "to join with" and in fuller writings is written with the feminine *t* ending; it means here "joined with Amun." Last is the feminine genitive *nt* and the word for "body," *ẖt*, which should have yet another *·(i)* added. It belongs with the word "daughter" and is a common way of talking about true bodily offspring "of [my] body."

7

7 "WORDS SPOKEN, 'I HAVE GIVEN TO YOU ALL STABILITY AND DOMINION, ALL HEALTH, ALL JOY, LIKE RE, FOREVER'" *ḏd mdw dỉ·n·(i) n·ṯ ḏd wꜣs nb snb nb ꜣwt-ỉb nb mỉ rꜥ ḏt (djed medu dieni netj djed was neb seneb neb aut-ib neb mi re djet)* You may notice that in place of *dỉ·n·(i) n·k* (see page 86) there is *dỉ·n·(i) n·ṯ*—the feminine suffix *·ṯ*, rather than the masculine *·k* (see page 48). This is an interesting example of the "femaleness" of Hatshepsut being acknowledged gramatically. Notions of Egyptian kingship did not allow for the ruler to be other than male, and it should be noted that in the picture the figure has no feminine attributes and wears the ritual royal beard. In some other texts relating to Hapshepsut, masculine grammatical forms are used; clearly those who composed the texts had problems reconciling her gender with her role as king. The remainder of the text is a series of items that the king is granting to the god—all seen in other inscriptions (see page 109).

III

III

PART THREE

REFERENCE FILE

SIGN LIST

Egyptologists classify hieroglyphs according to a system developed by Alan H. Gardiner in his *Egyptian Grammar* in 1927. The signs are divided into sections labelled A to Z and Aa. Within these groupings each sign is numbered: for example, the seated man, , is A1, the emblem of divinity, , is R8, and so on. The list that follows includes only those hieroglyphs shown in this book, with information on what each sign shows, its most common readings, use, and meanings. (Several sidebars provide some cultural information about additional signs.) The signs are orientated left to right. (For further guidance on using the sign list, see pages 34 to 36; for a comprehensive list and more information, readers should refer to Gardiner's book.)

A HUMAN BEINGS, MALE

	A1	**SEATED MAN** Suffix pronoun, first person singular, *ỉ*; determinative for "man" and "person"
	A2	**MAN WITH HAND TO MOUTH** Determinative for actions and emotions ("talk," "eat," "love," etc.)
	A8	**MAN IN ATTITUDE OF JUBILATION** Determinative for *hnw*, "praise," "jubilation," and in similar contexts
	A17	**CHILD** Determinative for "child;" word sign for *ẖrd*, "child"
	A30	**MAN WITH ARMS RAISED IN ADORATION** Determinative for "worship"
	A40	**SEATED GOD** Determinative for words associated with gods or kings
	A51	**SEATED MAN** Determinative for a dignitary or deceased person; word sign for *špss*, "noble"

B HUMAN BEINGS, FEMALE

 B1 **SEATED WOMAN** Determinative for woman, female

 B3 **WOMAN GIVING BIRTH** Determinative and word sign for *ms*, "give birth"

C ANTHROPOMORPHIC GODS

 C7 **SEATED SETH** Determinative or word sign for *stẖ*/*stš*, "Seth"

 C10 **SEATED GODDESS WITH FEATHER** Determinative or word sign for *mꜣꜥt*, "Maat". A variation of this sign holding an ankh is found .

D THE HUMAN BODY

 D1 **HEAD IN PROFILE** Word sign for *tp*, "head;" occasionally phonetic *tp*

 D2 **HEAD FROM FRONT** Word sign for *ḥr*, "face;" phonetic *ḥr*

 D4 **EYE** Determinative for eye-related words; phonetic *ỉr*

 D21 **MOUTH** Word sign for *r*, "mouth;" phonetic *r*

 D28 **UPRAISED ARMS** Word sign for *kꜣ*, "ka soul"; phonetic *kꜣ*

 D35 **PAIR OF ARMS** Determinative for negations; phonetic *n*, but only in negations

 D36 **ARM** Phonetic *ꜥ*

 D37 **ARM HOLDING LOAF X8** Phonetic *dỉ*, part of verb *rdỉ*

 D39 **ARM HOLDING POT** Determinative for "offer"

THE EYE OF HORUS

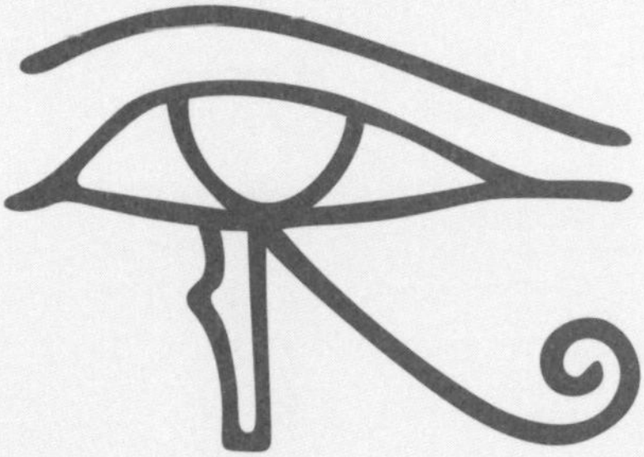

The *wedjat* ("sound one") is one of the oldest of hieroglyphs. Since the Old Kingdom, it took the form of the eye of the falcon-headed god Horus, which, according to myth, was ripped out by Seth during a battle over the inheritance of Osiris. The hieroglyph draws Horus's avian eye as a human one adorned by the curly plumage that grows beneath the eye of the lanner falcon. It is written as , *wḏꜣt* (*wedjat*), derived from a common word meaning "to be whole"—a reference to the act of reconstitution of the mutilated eye by the god Thoth. Thereafter the *wedjat* symbol promoted well-being for both the living and the dead, making it popular as an amulet.

The sign also has a mathematical usage. Its elements—the left white of the eye, pupil, eyebrow, right white, spiral, and the plumage beneath—form a set of fractions (beginning with $\frac{1}{2}$, then halving each time through to $\frac{1}{64}$) that combine, confusingly, to only $\frac{63}{64}$.

 D40 **ARM HOLDING STICK** Determinative for "force," "effort"

 D45 **ARM HOLDING A WAND** Phonetic *ḏsr*

 D46 **HAND** Phonetic *d*

 D50 **FINGER** Word sign for *ḏbꜥ*, "100,000" or "finger"

 D54 **LEGS** Determinative for motion (forward)

 D55 **LEGS** Determinative for motion (backward)

 D56 **LEG** Determinative for "foot," "leg"

 D58 **FOOT** Phonetic *b*

 D60 **FOOT WITH A VASE FROM WHICH WATER IS FLOWING** Word sign for *wab*, "clean," and "pure"

E MAMMALS

 E1 **BULL** Determinative and word sign for "bull," "ox," and "cattle"

 E10 **RAM** Word sign for *ẖnmw*, "Khnum"

 E17 **JACKAL** Determinative and word sign for *zꜣb*, "judge," and "jackal"

 E20 **SETH ANIMAL** Determinative and word sign for *stẖ/stš*, "Seth"

 E21 **SETH ANIMAL** Determinative and word sign for *stẖ/stš*, "Seth"

 E23 **RECUMBENT LION** Phonetic *rw*

 E34 **HARE** Phonetic *wn*

F PARTS OF MAMMALS

	F1	**HEAD OF OX** Word sign for *kꜣ* and *ỉḥ*, "oxen" and "cattle;" F1 in the offering formula is usually *kꜣ*
	F4	**FOREPARTS OF LION** Strictly speaking a word sign for *ḥꜥt*, "front," and so on, but can be thought of as phonetic *ḥꜣt*
	F9	**HEAD OF LEOPARD** Determinative and word sign for *pḥty*, "strength"
	F12	**HEAD AND NECK OF CANINE ANIMAL** Phonetic *wsr*
	F13	**HORNS OF OX** Phonetic *wp*
	F14	**COMBINATION OF F13 AND M4** Used in *wpt-rnpt*, "New Year's Day"
	F17	**HORN WITH WATER POT** Determinative and word sign for *ꜥbw*, "purification"
	F20	**OX-TONGUE [?]** Determinative for tongue actions; phonetic *ns*; abbreviation for *ỉmy-r*, "overseer"
	F21	**EAR OF OX** Determinative for "ear"; phonetic *sḏm*
	F23	**LEG OF AN OX** Determinative and word sign for *ḫpš*, "ox foreleg"
	F24	**LEG OF AN OX REVERSED** As F23
	F25	**LEG AND HOOF OF OX** Phonetic *wḥm*
	F29	**COW'S SKIN PIERCED BY ARROW** Determinative and word sign for "pierce;" phonetic *st* in *stt*, goddess "Satet"
	F30	**WATER-SKIN** Phonetic *šd*
	F31	**ANIMAL SKINS** Phonetic *ms*
	F32	**ANIMAL'S BELLY WITH TEATS** Word sign for "belly" and "body;" phonetic *ẖ*

F34 **OX HEART** Word sign for *ỉb*, "heart"

F35 **HEART AND WINDPIPE** Phonetic *nfr* was used to express "perfect," "happy," "good," and so on

F36 **LUNG AND WINDPIPE** Phonetic *smꜣ*

F39 **RIBS** Determinative and word sign for *ỉmꜣḫ*, "honor"

F40 **RIBS** Phonetic *ꜣw*

F46 **INTESTINES [ALSO F47, F48, F49]** Determinative and word sign for "turn round" and "intestine"; phonetic *pḫr* in *pḫr*, "turn"

F51 **PIECE OF MEAT** Determinative for "flesh"

G BIRDS

G1 **EGYPTIAN VULTURE** Phonetic *ꜣ*. [Not to be confused with G4]

G4 **LONG-LEGGED BUZZARD** Phonetic *tyw*. [Not to be confused with G1]

G5 **FALCON** Word sign for *ḥr*, "Horus"

G7 **FALCON ON DIVINE PERCH** Determinative for "divine," with gods and kings.

G9 **FALCON WITH SUN DISC** Combined word signs for *rꜥ* and *ḥr* in *rꜥ-ḥr-ꜥḫty*, "Re-Horakhty"

G14 **VULTURE** Phonetic *mwt*, esp. in *mwt*, "mother" and goddess "Mut"

G16 **VULTURE AND COBRA ON BASKETS** Word sign for *nbty*, "two ladies" (see page 38)

G17 **OWL** Phonetic *m*

G21 **GUINEA-FOWL** Phonetic *nḥ*

 G26 **IBIS ON PERCH** Word sign for *ḏḥwty*, "Thoth"

 G28 **BLACK IBIS** Phonetic *gm*

 G29 **JABIRU** Word sign for *bꜣ*, "ba-spirit"; phonetic *bꜣ*

 G30 **JABIRU TRIPLED AS MONOGRAM** Word sign for *bꜣw*, "spirits," and "ba-spirits"

 G47 **DUCKLING** Phonetic *tꜣ*

 G36 **SWALLOW OR MARTIN** [Not to be confused with G37] Phonetic *wr*

 G37 **SPARROW** [Not to be confused with G36] Determinative for "small," "bad"

 G38 **WHITE-FRONTED GOOSE** Determinative for "bird;" phonetic *gb* in "Geb"

 G39 **PINTAIL DUCK** [Not to be confused with much rarer G38] Phonetic *zꜣ*

 G43 **QUAIL CHICK** Phonetic *w*

H PARTS OF BIRDS

 H1 **HEAD OF DUCK** Word sign for *ꜣpd*, "bird"

 H6 **FEATHER** Determinative and word sign for *mꜣꜥt*, "maat"

 H8 **EGG** Here used as a determinative for some goddesses' names (for example, *ꜣst*, "Isis")

I REPTILES

 I4 **CROCODILE ON SHRINE** Determinative and word sign for *sbk*, "Sebek"

 I6 **CROCODILE SCALES** Phonetic *km*

 I9 **HORNED VIPER** Phonetic *f*

 I10 **COBRA IN REPOSE** Phonetic *ḏ*

 I12 **ERECT COBRA (AS ON THE ROYAL URAEUS)** Determinative for words meaning "uraeus" and also for female deities in snake form, notably Wadjet, protective goddess of Lower Egypt

K FISHES

 K1 **TILAPIA** Determinative for "fish" and similar; phonetic *in*

L INSECTS

 L1 **SCARAB** Phonetic *ḫpr*

 L2 **BEE** Word sign for *bity*, "king of Lower Egypt"

M VEGETATION

 M2 **HERB** Determinative for "flower;" phonetic *ḥn*

 M3 **STICK** Determinative for "stick" and "wood;" phonetic *ḫt*

 M4 **PALM BRANCH** Word sign for *rnpt*, "year;" used in "regnal year"

 M12 **LEAF, STALK, AND RHIZOME OF LILY** Word sign for *ḫꜣ*, "1,000;" phonetic *ḫꜣ*

 M13 **STEM OF PAPYRUS** Phonetic *wꜣḏ*, but can also read *wḏ*

 M16 **CLUMP OF PAPYRUS** Phonetic *ḥꜣ*

 M17 **FLOWERING REED** Phonetic *ỉ*; when doubled, phonetic *y*

 M18 **FLOWERING REED WITH LEGS (M17 AND D54)** Phonetic *ỉ* in verb *ỉy*, "to come"

 M20 **REEDS GROWING SIDE BY SIDE** Word sign for *sẖt* , "field," and "land"

 M23 **UPPER EGYPTIAN PLANT, POSSIBLY SEDGE** Phonetic *sw*; common abbreviation for *nswt*, "king"

THE MANY MEANINGS OF THE LILY

The water lily played an important role in religious iconography. In one Egyptian creation myth, the creator god appeared on top of a lily that was growing on the primeval waters. The flower therefore became a symbol of transformation and rebirth—an association with new life that linked it to fertility and sexuality. There are many examples of tomb paintings in which people (primarily women) are depicted at banquets inhaling fragrance from the lily. According to Egyptian symbolism, this act expresses the desire for life after death. Lilies also appear on the capitals of columns in Egyptian temples—in this context they represent the primeval vegetation from which the world was created.

M24 **COMBINATION OF M23 AND D21** Phonetic *rsw* or *rsy* in words meaning "south"

M26 **FLOWERING SEDGE PLANT** Phonetic *šmꜥ* in *šmꜥyt*, "singer"; also in *šmꜥ(w)*, Upper Egypt

M27 **COMBINATION OF M26 AND D36** Mostly interchangeable with M26

M36 **BUNDLE OF FLAX** Phonetic *ḏr*

M41 **LOG OF WOOD** Determinative for "wood"

M44 **THORN** Determinative for "thorn," "sharp;" possibly phonetic *spd*, particularly *spdt*, goddess "Sopdet/Sirius"

N SKY, EARTH, WATER

N1 **SKY** Determinative and word sign for sky and above, especially in *pt*, "sky," and "heaven"

N5 **SUN DISC** Determinative and word sign for "sun," "day;" esp. word sign for *rꜥ*, "sun," "sun-disc," and "Re"

N7 **SUN DISC WITH BUTCHER'S BLOCK** Word sign for *ḫrt-hrw*, "daytime," and "course of day"

N8 **SUNSHINE** Determinative for "sunlight"; phonetic *wbn*

N11 **CRESCENT MOON** Word sign for *ꜣbd*, "month," in dates; phonetic and determinative for *iꜥḥ*, "moon"; perhaps for reasons of phonetic similarity, used in *wꜥḥ*, "carob bean"

N14 **STAR** Determinative "star"; phonetic *sbꜣ*, as in "star;" phonetic *dwꜣ*, as in "worship"

N16 **LAND WITH GRAINS OF SAND** Word sign for *tꜣ*, "land" and "earth;" phonetic *tꜣ*

N17 **N16 WITHOUT SAND** As N16

N18 **SANDY TRACT** Determinative for "desert," "foreign land;" word sign for *iw*, "island;" here used mostly in N19

N19 **TWO SANDY TRACTS** Word sign for *ꜣḫt*, "horizon," in name of gods, *ḥr-ꜣḫty*, "Horakhty," and *rꜥ-ḥr-ꜣḫty*, "Re-Horakhty"

N21 **TONGUE OF LAND** Determinative for "land"

N24 **LAND MARKED OUT WITH IRRIGATION CHANNELS** Determinative for some province names and districts within Egypt

N25 **SANDY HILL-COUNTRY OVER EDGE OF CULTIVATION** Determinative for "desert" and "foreign land;" word sign for *ḫꜣst*, "desert" and "foreign land"

N26 **SAND-COVERED MOUNTAIN OVER EDGE OF CULTIVATION** Word sign for *ḏw*, "mountain;" phonetic *ḏw*

N27 **SUN RISING OVER MOUNTAIN** Word sign for *ꜣḫt*, "horizon"

N28 **SUN RISING OVER HILL** Phonetic *ḫꜥ*, esp. *ḫꜥ*, "appear"

N29 **SANDY SLOPE** Phonetic *q*

N33 **GRAIN OF SAND** Determinative for "sand," "mineral," "pellet." When tripled, an alternative to the plural strokes Z2 and Z3

N35 **WATER** Phonetic *n*

N36 **CHANNEL FILLED WITH WATER** Determinative for "body of water;" phonetic *mr*

N37 **GARDEN POOL** Phonetic *š*

N41 **WELL FULL OF WATER** Phonetic *ḥm*

N42 **ALTERNATIVE FORM OF N41** See N41

O STRUCTURES

O1 **HOUSE** Determinative for "building;" word sign for *pr*, "house;" phonetic *pr*

O3 **O1 COMBINED WITH P8, X3, W22** Word sign for *prt-ḫrw*, "invocation offering"

O4 **SHELTER** Phonetic *h*

O6 **RECTANGULAR ENCLOSURE IN PLAN** Word sign for *ḥwt*, "enclosure," "mansion," "estate"

O7 **ALTERNATIVE FORM OF O6** See O6

O9 **COMBINATION OF O7 AND V30** Word sign for *nbt-ḥwt*, "Nephthys"

O10 **COMBINATION OF O6 AND G5** Word sign for *ḥwt-ḥr*, "Hathor"

O20 **SHRINE** Determinative for "shrine"

O22 **OPEN BOOTH SUPPORTED BY A POLE** Determinative for *zḥ*, "counsel," "advice," and *zḥ*, "booth," "tent;" here used mostly with W4

O29 **COLUMN** Phonetic *ꜥꜣ*

O34 **BOLT** Phonetic *z*; later can be used for *s* (S29)

O42 **FENCE** Phonetic *šzp*

O47 **PREHISTORIC BUILDING AT HIERAKONPOLIS** Word sign for *nḫn*, "Nekhen," "Hierakonpolis"

O48 **ALTERNATIVE FORM OF O47** See O47

O49 **TOWN CROSSROADS** Determinative for "town," "city;" word sign for *niwt*, "town"

O50 **THRESHING FLOOR** Phonetic *zp*

P SHIPS AND PARTS OF SHIPS

P1 **BOAT** Determinative and word sign for "boat"; there are many words for "boat," of which *dpt* is the most common

P6 **MAST** Phonetic *ꜥḥꜥ*

P8 **OAR** Phonetic *ḫrw*, particularly used in *mꜣꜥ-ḫrw*, "true of voice"

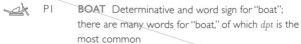

VEHICLES OF THE GODS

When gods are depicted in Egyptian art taking part in festivals, the figure of the god is often in a shrine on a boat that is being carried on the shoulders of priests. Similarly, when the sun god is shown traveling across the sky or through the underworld (as in the statue on page 110), he stands in a boat. The Nile river was the life artery of ancient Egypt, and boats were the primary means of transport on longer journeys, so it is perhaps unsurprising that the deities were imagined as voayaging in this way. A typical depiction of a funeral in an Egyptian tomb would include the deceased's coffin crossing the river in a boat from the east (representing life) to the west (representing death).

Q DOMESTIC AND FUNERARY FURNITURE

𓊨 Q1 **SEAT** Phonetic *st*; also commonly found here in *ȝst*, "Isis," 𓊨𓏏𓁐 and *wsir*, "Osiris," 𓁹𓊨𓀭

𓊩 Q2 **PORTABLE SEAT** Often used in place of Q1 in *wsir*, "Osiris"

𓊪 Q3 **STOOL OF REED MATTING** Phonetic *p*

R TEMPLE FURNITURE AND SACRED EMBLEMS

R3 **TABLE WITH FOOD AND LIBATION VASE** Determinative and word sign for *wḏḥw*, "offering table"

R4 **LOAF ON REED MAT** Phonetic *ḥtp*

R7 **BOWL FOR INCENSE WITH SMOKE RISING** Determinative and word sign for *snṯr*, "incense"

R8 **CLOTH WOUND ON A POLE, DIVINE PENNANT** Word sign for *nṯr*, "god;" phonetic *nṯr*

R11 **COLUMN IMITATING BUNDLE OF STALKS TIED TOGETHER** Phonetic *ḏd*

R12 **STYLIZED PERCH WITH FEATHER** Usually used with other signs

R14 **FEATHER ON STANDARD** Word sign for *ỉmnt*, "west"

R15 **SPEAR AS A STANDARD** Word sign for *ỉꜣbt*, "east"

R19 **S40 WITH FEATHER** Word sign for *wꜣst*, "Thebes"

S REGALIA AND CLOTHING

S1 **WHITE CROWN** Word sign for *ḥḏt*, "white crown;" determinative for words representing this

S3 **RED CROWN** Phonetic *n* (N35 more common); determinative for words representing "red crown"

S5 **COMBINED WHITE AND RED CROWNS** Determinative for "crown" and words representing "double crown;" word sign for *sḫmty*, "double crown"

S10 **CLOTH HEADBAND** Determinative for "headband;" phonetic *mḏḥ*

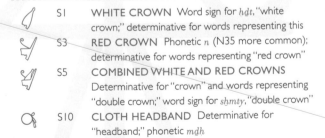

S12 **COLLAR OF BEADS** Determinative for "precious metals;" word sign for *nbw*, "gold"

S24 **GIRDLE KNOT** Phonetic *ṯz*

S27 **STRIP OF CLOTH WITH TWO STRANDS OF A FRINGE** Determinative and word sign for *mnḫt*, "cloth"

S28 **STRIP OF CLOTH WITH FRINGE, COMBINED WITH S29** Determinative for "cloth," "clothing"

S29 **FOLDED CLOTH** Phonetic *s*

S34 **SANDAL STRAP [?]** Phonetic *ꜥnḫ*

S38 **CROOK** Phonetic *ḥqꜣ*

S40 **SCEPTER WITH HEAD OF SETH ANIMAL [?]** Phonetic *wꜣs*

S42 **SCEPTER OF AUTHORITY** In this book, used as a determinative or word sign for *ḫrp*, "controller;" phonetically mainly *sḫm*, but can be *ꜥbꜣ*.

S43 **WALKING STICK** Phonetic *md*

T WARFARE, HUNTING, BUTCHERY

T3 **MACE WITH PEAR-SHAPED HEAD** Phonetic *ḥḏ*

T8 **DAGGER** Phonetic *tp*

T11 **ARROW** Determinative and word sign for *šsr*, "arrow;" used for a type of linen (*šsr*)

T12 **BOW STRING** Phonetic *rwḏ*

T13 **PIECES OF WOOD JOINED AND LASHED** Phonetic *rs*

 T14 **ALTERNATIVE FORM OF T15** See T15

 T15 **THROW-STICK OR CLUB** Determinative for "foreign," esp. in names, such as *ṯḥnw*, "Libya," and also as determinative or word signs in words for throwstick; also features in *ṯḥnw*, "tjehenu oil"

 T21 **HARPOON** Phonetic *wꜥ*

 T22 **TWO-BARBED ARROWHEAD** Phonetic *sn*

 T23 **ALTERNATIVE FORM OF T22** New Kingdom version

 T28 **BUTCHER'S BLOCK** Phonetic *ẖr*

U AGRICULTURE, CRAFTS, AND PROFESSIONS

 U1 **SICKLE** Phonetic *mꜣ*

 U2 **ALTERNATIVE FORM OF U1** See U1

 U3 **SICKLE WITH D4** Phonetic *mꜣ*, especially in "see"

 U4 **SICKLE WITH Aa11** Phonetic *mꜣꜥ*

 U5 **ALTERNATIVE FORM OF U4** See U4

 U6 **HOE** Phonetic *mr*

 U7 **ALTERNATIVE FORM OF U6** See U6

 U21 **ADZE ON A BLOCK OF WOOD** Phonetic *stp*

 U23 **CHISEL [?]** Phonetic *mr*, *ꜣb*

 U24 **STONE WORKER'S BAG DRILL** Word sign for "craft," esp. in *ḥmt*, "craftsman"

 U28 **FIRE-DRILL** Phonetic *ḏꜣ*

 U30 **KILN** Phonetic *tꜣ*

 U33 **PESTLE** Phonetic *tỉ*

 U34 **SPINDLE** Phonetic *ḫsf*

 U36 **CLUB** Phonetic *ḥm*

V ROPE, BASKETS, AND CLOTH

 V1 **COIL OF ROPE** Determinative for "rope;" word sign for *št*, "100"

 V4 **LASSO** Phonetic *wꜣ*

 V6 **CORD WITH ENDS UP** Phonetic *šs* or *šsr*

 V7 **CORD WITH ENDS DOWN** Phonetic *šn*

 V12 **BAND OF STRING OR LINEN** Determinative for "bind," "papyrus book"

 V13 **TETHERING ROPE** Phonetic *ṯ*

 V14 **TETHERING ROPE WITH ADDED TICK** See V13

 V15 **TETHERING ROPE WITH D54** Phonetic *ỉṯ*

 V17 **ROLLED UP PAPYRUS SHELTER** Phonetic *zꜣ*

 V20 **CATTLE HOBBLE** Word sign for *md*, "10"

 V22 **WHIP** Phonetic *mḥ*

 V24 **CORD WOUND ON STICK** Phonetic *wḏ*

V28 **WICK OF TWISTED FLAX** Phonetic *ḥ*

V29 **HANK OF FIBER** Phonetic *wꜣḥ*, *sk*

V30 **BASKET** Phonetic *nb*

V31 **BASKET WITH HANDLE** Phonetic *k*

V31 **BASKET WITH HANDLE (REVERSED)** As V31; usually only used in modern hieroglyphic transcriptions of hieratic, where the handle faces the front

V33 **BAG OF LINEN** Determinative for "bag;" occasionally phonetic *g*

W STONE AND CERAMIC VESSELS

W1 **SEALED OIL-JAR** Determinative for "oil;" sometimes used as word sign for *mrḥt*, "merhet oil"

W2 **SEALED OIL-JAR** Variant of W1; one use is in the name *bꜣstt*, "Bastet"

W3 **BASIN** Word sign for *ḥb*, "feast"

W4 **BASIN WITH O22** As W3

W5 **W3 AND T28** Word sign for *ẖry-ḥb*, "lector priest"

W9 **STONE JUG** Phonetic *ẖnm*

W10 **CUP** Determinative for "cup;" phonetic *ḥnw* in words such as *ḥnwt*, "mistress"

W11 **JAR STAND** Determinative or word sign for *nst*, "seat," and "throne;" phonetic *g*; phonetic *ns*

W14 **TALL WATER POT** Phonetic *ḥz*

W15 **WATER POT POURING WATER** Determinative or word sign for "cool," such as *qbḥ*, "cool water"

W16 **W15 WITH SPOUT IN STAND W12** As W15

W17 **WATER POTS IN A RACK** Phonetic *ḫnt*

W19 **VESSEL CARRIED IN NET** Phonetic *mỉ*

W22 **BEER JUG** Determinative for "pot"; determinative or word sign for *ḥnqt*, "beer," esp. in offering formulas

W24 **BOWL** Phonetic *nw*; for unknown reason, often accompanies Aa27

W25 **COMBINATION OF W24 AND D54** Phonetic *ỉn*, esp. *ỉn*, "to bring," "to fetch"

X BREAD

X1 **BREAD** Phonetic *t*

X2 **LOAF** Determinative for "bread," "food;" word sign for *t*, "bread," in offering formulas

X4 **BREAD ROLL** Determinative for "bread," "food"

X8 **CONICAL LOAF** Phonetic *dỉ* in parts of verb *rdỉ*, "to give"

Y WRITINGS, GAMES, AND MUSIC

Y1 **ROLLED-UP PAPYRUS, BOOK-ROLL** Determinative for writing, abstract concepts

Y3 **SCRIBE'S OUTFIT** Word sign for scribal matters, in particular, *zš*, "write," and "scribe"

Y5 **GAME-BOARD** Phonetic *mn*

Z STROKES AND FIGURES

Z1 **STROKE** Placed with signs serving primarily as word signs rather than being primarily phonetic Also word sign for *wꜥ*, "I"

Z2 **STROKE TRIPLED (HORIZONTAL)** Plural strokes

Z3 **STROKE TRIPLED (VERTICAL)** As Z2

Z4 **TWO DIAGONAL STROKES** Phonetic *y*

Z7 **HIEROGLYPHIC ADAPTATION OF THE HIERATIC ABBREVIATED FORM OF G43** Phonetic *w*; only really found after the middle Eighteenth Dynasty

Z11 **TWO PLANKS CROSSED AND JOINED** Phonetic *im*

Aa UNCLASSIFIED

Aa1 **HUMAN PLACENTA [?]** Phonetic *ḫ*

Aa2 **PUSTULE OR GLAND** Determinative for "swelling," "unhealthy," and in *wt*, "bandage"; used differently as a determinative in some words

Aa5 **PART OF STEERING GEAR OF SHIPS [?]** Phonetic *hp*

Aa7 **UNKNOWN** Determinative for *sqr*, "smite"

Aa11 **UNKNOWN** Phonetic *mꜣꜥ*, esp. in *mꜣꜥt*, "truth," and related words

Aa13 **UNKNOWN** See Aa15

Aa15 **UNKNOWN, RIBS [?]** Phonetic *m*

Aa17 **BACK OF SOMETHING [?]** Phonetic *sꜣ*

Aa27 **UNKNOWN** Phonetic *nḏ*

SHAPE LIST

Although it is often apparent what a hieroglyph is showing—for example,  can be found in group A (Human beings, male)—some signs cannot be identified easily. Gardiner therefore also developed a "shape list." In this adapted form of the list, the signs are in three groups. Search by the shape, then next to the sign you will find the Gardiner number, which enables you to locate it in the main sign list.

TALL, NARROW SIGNS

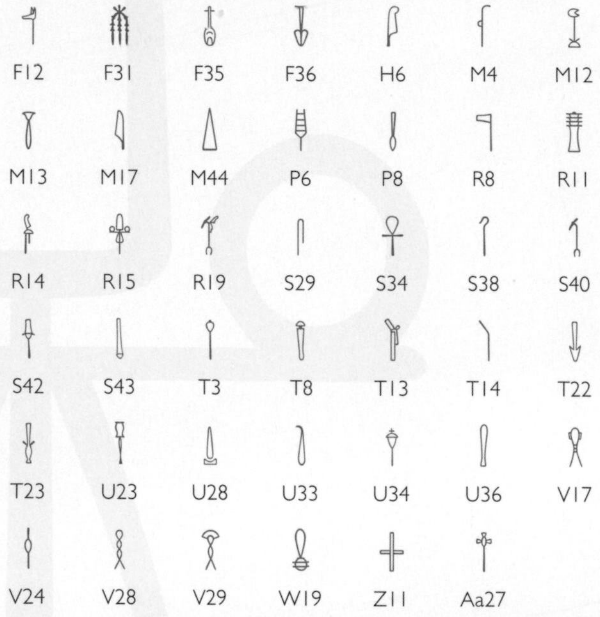
F12 F31 F35 F36 H6 M4 M12
M13 M17 M44 P6 P8 R8 R11
R14 R15 R19 S29 S34 S38 S40
S42 S43 T3 T8 T13 T14 T22
T23 U23 U28 U33 U34 U36 V17
V24 V28 V29 W19 Z11 Aa27

LOW, BROAD SIGNS

D21	F20	F32	F46	N1	N11	N17
N18	N35	N36	N37	O29	O34	O42
R4	S24	T11	T21	U21	V13	V14
V22	V30	V31	V31	W3	X4	Aa7
Aa15						

LOW, NARROW SIGNS

F34	H8	I6	M36	M41	N5	N8
N28	N29	N33	N41	N42	O47	O48
O49	O50	Q3	R7	T28	U30	V1
V6	V7	V20	V33	W10	W11	X2
Z7	Aa1	Aa2	Aa17			

VOCABULARY LIST

This short vocabulary includes most of the words used in this book. But for more comprehensive listings, specialized works should be consulted, such as those mentioned in Further Reading.

As will be evident by now, ancient Egyptian writings are inconsistent. Many of the words here are therefore written in more than one way, but only in order to reflect the forms used in the examples. Parts of speech are given next to the words and are abbreviated as (n) noun, (v) verb, (av) adverb, (a) adjective, (p) preposition. All words are in left-to-right orientation.

HIEROGLYPHS	TRANSLITERATION AND MEANING
	*ꜣwt-ỉb* joy (n)
	*ꜣbd* month (n)
	*ꜣbḏw* Abydos (n)
	*ꜣpd* bird, fowl (n)
	*ꜣḫt* horizon (n)
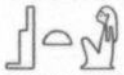	*ꜣst* Isis (n)
	*ỉ* I, my (suffix pronoun)
	*ỉꜣbt* east (n); later *ỉꜣbtt*
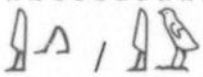	*ỉy* to come; the special form *ỉyw* with a dative means "welcome"—a short form of "come to me" (v)
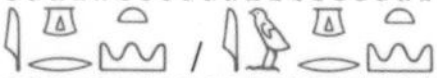	*ỉwgrt* I(u)gret (n)

ỉb heart (n)

ỉp to count (v)

ỉm there (av)

ỉmꜣḫ honored one (n)

ỉmy-r overseer (n)

ỉmn Amun (n)

ỉmnt west (n)

ỉmsty Imsety (n, son of Horus)

ỉn by (p)

ỉnk I (at beginning of clause—independent pronoun; see page 46)

ỉr to do, to make (v)

ỉḥ ox (n)

ỉt father (n)

ꜥꜣ great (a)

ꜥb purification libation (n)

ꜥnḫ life; to live; living (n, v, a)

ꜥš cedar (n)

---

wꜣs dominion (n)

wꜣst Thebes (n)

wꜥ one (cardinal number)

wꜥb pure (a)

	*wꜥḥ* carob bean (n)
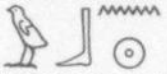	*wbn* to rise (v)
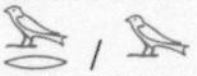	*wr* great (a)
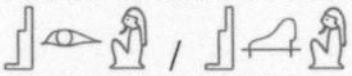	*wsỉr* Osiris (n)
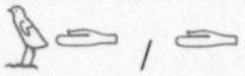	*wḏ* to give, to put, to present (v)
	*wḏḥw* offering table (n)
	*bꜣw* spirits, particularly ba-spirits (n)
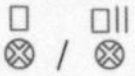	*p* Pe, Egyptian name for Buto, modern Kom Faraun in the Delta (n)
	*pr* house (n)
	*pr* to go out, to come forth (v)
	*prt-ḫrw* invocations offerings, to make invocation offerings (n, v)
	*pḥty* strength (n)
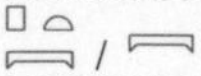	*pt* sky, heaven (n)
	*f* he, his (suffix pronoun)
	*m* in, through (p)
	*mꜣꜥ-ḫrw* justified (having successfully passed the Judgment of the Dead) (a)

	*mꜣꜥt* truth, right; Maat (goddess) (n)
	*mỉ* like (p)
	*mwt* mother (n)
	*mn* to establish, established (v, a)
	*mnṯw* Montu (n)
	*mr* to love (v); *mry*, "beloved" (n, a)
	*mrḥt* merhet oil (n)
	*mḥ* cubit (n)
	*ms* to give birth, to be born (v); *mswt*, "births" (n)
	*mdw* word (n)
	*mḏḥ* headband (n)

	*n* of (genitive); to, for (dative); *nt* feminine genitive (p)
	*n* we, our (suffix pronoun)
	*nb* all, every (a)
	*nb* lord, master (n); *nb ỉr ḫt* "lord of cult action"; occasionally written with a recumbent lion , or sphinx
	*nbt* lady, mistress (n)
	*nbty* Two Ladies (royal name) (n)
	*nbt-ḥwt* Nephthys (n)

	*nfr* good, perfect (a)
	*nḥḥ* eternity (n)
	*nḫn* Nekhen, Greek Hierakonpolis, modern Kom el-Ahmar in Upper Egypt (n)
	*nḫnm* nekhenem oil (n)
	*nswt* king (n)
	*nswt-bỉty* king of Upper and Lower Egypt (n)
	*nṯr* god (n)
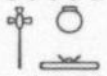	*nḏ* to avenge; avenger (v, n)

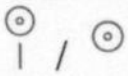	*rʿ* sun, day; with determinative , "Re," the sun god (n)
	*rʿ-ḥr-ꜣḫty* Re-Horakhty (n)
	*rn* name (n)
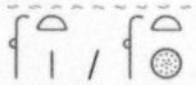	*rnpt* year (n); *rnpt zp*, "regnal year"
	*rḫ* to know (v)
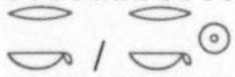	*rk* time, age ("the expanse of time") (n)
	*rdỉ*/ *dỉ* to give (v)
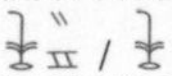	*rsy* south (n); southern (a)

	*hnw* / *hny* rejoice, jubilation (v, n)

	*ḥꜣtt* best, as in *ḥꜣtt-ꜥš* or *ḥꜣtt ṯḥnw* "best cedar oil," "best tjehnu oil" (n)
	*ḥꜥ* limb, flesh (n)
	*ḥwn* youth (n)
	*ḥwt-ḥr* Hathor (n)
	*ḥpy* Hapy (n, son of Horus)
	*ḥpw* Apis bull (n)
	*ḥfn* one hundred thousand (cardinal number)
	*ḥm* servant; in relation to king, "majesty of" (n)
	*ḥm-nṯr* priest ("god's servant") (n)
	*ḥmt* wife; *ḥmt nswt wrt*, great royal wife (n)
	*ḥnwt* mistress (n)
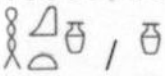	*ḥnqt* beer (n)
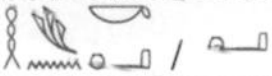	*ḥnk* to offer (v)
	*ḥr* face (n)
	*ḥr* Horus (n)
	*ḥr* Upon (p)
	*ḥr-ꜣḫty* Horakhty (n)
	*ḥr-ib* in the heart of; with gods, "who dwells in" (relative pronoun)
	*ḥr-tp* foremost (a)

	*ḥḥ* million (cardinal number)
	see *nḥḥ*, eternity
	*ḥqꜣ* ruler (n)
	*ḥknw* heknu oil (n)
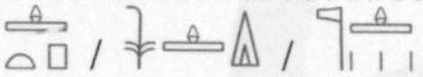	*ḥtp* offering; most common here in *ḥtp di nswt* "an offering which the king gives;" also in *ḥtp-nṯrw*, "divine offerings" (n); peace (n)

	*ḫꜣ* thousand (cardinal number)
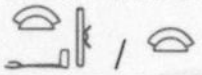	*ḫꜥ* to appear; appearance (v, n)
	*ḫpr* to come into existence; form (v, n)
	*ḫpš* leg of an ox (n)
	*ḫft* in accordance with (p); when (conjunction)
	*ḫnty* foremost (a); with god, "who dwells in" (relative pronoun)
	*ḫnd* leg; to tread (n, v)
	*ḫr* before (p)
	*ḫrp* controller (n)
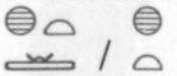	*ḫt* thing, property (n)

	*ẖry-ḥb* lector priest (n)
	*ẖrt-hrw* in the course of (time) (p)

	*ẖrd* child (n)

	*zȝ* son (n)
	*zȝb* judge (legal title) (n)
	*zȝt* daughter (n)
	*zp* occasion (n)
	*zmȝ* *to* unify (v); *zmȝ-tȝwy*, "unifying the two lands" (v)
	*zš* scribe; to write (n, v)

	*s* she, her (suffix pronoun)
	*swty* Seth (n)
	*sbk* Sobek (crocodile god) (n)
	*sfṯ* seftj oil (n)
	*sm* sem priest (who usually wears a leopard skin) (n)
	*sn* two (cardinal number)
	*sn* brother (n)
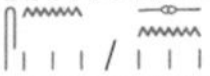	*sn* they, their (suffix pronoun)
	*snb* health (n)
	*snt* sister (n)
	*snṯr* incense (n)
	*sẖt* field, area of land (particularly marshland) (n)

	*sšr* clothing (n)
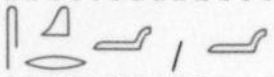	*sqr* to smite (v)
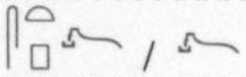	*stp* to choose; chosen (v, a)
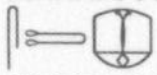	*sṯ-ḥb* setj-heb oil (n)
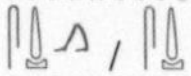	*sḏꜣ* to proceed (v)

	*šmʿyt* singer (n)
	*šs* Egyptian alabaster (n)
	šsr a type of linen (n); arrow (n)
	*št* or *šnt* hundred (cardinal number)
	*šdt* Crocodilopolis (n)

	*qbḥ-snw·f* Qebehsenuef (n, son of Horus)

	*k* you, your (masc. sing. suffix pronoun)
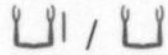	*kꜣ* ka soul (n)

	*t* bread (n)
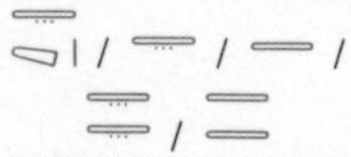	*tꜣ* land; *tꜣwy* "the Two Lands" (Upper and Lower Egypt) (n)
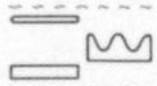	*tꜣ-š* the Faiyum region (n)
	*twꜣ* tua oil (n)
	*twt* image, statue (n)

	*tp* head (n)
	*tpy* first (a)

	*ṯ* you, your (fem. sing. suffix pronoun)
	*ṯn* you, your (plural suffix pronoun)
	*ṯḥnw* tjehnu oil (n)
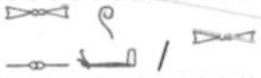	*ṯz* to tie (v)
	*ṯz-pẖr* expression "and the reverse," "vice-versa" (see page 89)

	see *wd*
	see *rdi*
	*dwꜣ* to worship, to adore (v)
	*dwꜣ-mwt·f* Duamutef (n, son of Horus)

	*ḏbꜥ* ten thousand (cardinal number)
	*ḏḥwty* Thoth (n)
	*ḏsr* holy (a)
	*ḏt* eternity (n)
	*ḏd* to speak (v)
	*ḏd* stability (n)
	*ḏdw* Busiris (n)
	*ḏd-mdw* recitation, words spoken (n)

FURTHER READING

GRAMMARS AND DICTIONARIES

Rather than alphabetical order, these grammar books and dictionaries are arranged in a sequence that will enable the reader to make gradual steps toward the mastery of hieroglyphs.

How to Read Egyptian Hieroglyphs, by Mark Collier and Bill Manley *(British Museum Press, 1998; rpt. 2003)*
If you have been able to work your way though this book with success, then you do not need most of the more popular publications out there. An intermediate step might be this book, which takes a systematic approach, with exercises. It uses a range of texts from the collections of the British Museum. Readers should note that this book uses a non-standard numbering of the hieroglyphs.

Middle Egyptian, by J. P. Allen *(Cambridge University Press, 2000)*
Further progress can be made by acquiring one of the grammar books used by university students. This is the most up-to-date example in English, complete with exercises and plenty of reference material.

Egyptian Grammar, by A. H. Gardiner *(Griffith Institute, 3rd ed., 1957)*
Still in print, this was for many years the standard reference work, although the second half, on verbs, is now largely outdated. But it does have exercises, and contains the full sign list used as a basis for the excerpts in this book. Every aspiring Egyptologist should have a copy on their shelves.

A Concise Dictionary of Middle Egyptian, by R. O. Faulkner *(Griffith Institute, 1962)*
Another essential work as you move away from the grammar books is a dictionary, and this is the book you need.

Wörterbuch der Ägyptischen Sprache, by A. Erman and H. Grapow *(Leipzig, Hinrichs, 1926–1951)*
Once you become more advanced, you will need access to this seven-volume standard dictionary of Egyptian. Although now no longer in print, and outdated, it can be found in any Egyptological library. Egyptology conducted at this level requires a knowledge of English, German, and French.

TRANSLATIONS OF EGYPTIAN TEXTS

Ancient Egyptian Literature, volumes I–III, by M. Lichtheim *(University of California Press, 1973–1980; rpt. 2006)*
This is the most wide-ranging selection (by date) of Egyptian stories and other literary texts.

The Tale of Sinuhe and Other Ancient Egyptian Poems, 1940–1640 BC, by R. B. Parkinson *(Oxford, World's Classics, 1997; rpt. 2009)*
These are the most recent translations of the famous Middle Egyptian texts.

GENERAL CULTURAL WORKS

The Keys of Egypt, by L. and R. Adkins *(HarperCollins, 2001)*

The Cultural Atlas of Ancient Egypt, by J. Baines and J. Malek *(Facts on File, 2000)*

The Routledge Dictionary of Egyptian Gods and Goddesses, by G. Hart *(Routledge, 2005)*

Egyptian Mythology: A Guide to the Gods, Goddesses, and Traditions of Ancient Egypt, by G. Pinch *(Oxford University Press, 2004)*

Ancient Egyptian Religion, by S. Quirke *(British Museum Press, 1992 & Dover Publications, 1993)*

The Art of Ancient Egypt, by G. Robins *(British Museum Press & Harvard University Press, rev. ed., 2008)*

Egypt: The World of the Pharaohs, by R. Schulz and M. Seidel *(Koenemann, 1998)*

The Oxford History of Ancient Egypt, by I. Shaw (general editor) *(Oxford University Press, 2003)*

Ancient Egypt, by D. P. Silverman (general editor) *(Duncan Baird Publishers & Oxford University Press, 1997; rev. ed., 2003)*

Death and the Afterlife in Ancient Egypt, by J. H. Taylor *(British Museum Press & University of Chicago Press, 2001)*

INDEX

References to picture captions are in *italics*

ACKNOWLEDGMENTS AND PICTURE CREDITS

Author Acknowledgments

I would like to thank Helen Strudwick for help and support, and in particular for commenting on the text and checking the lists. Cleo Huggins I thank for permitting me many years ago to use her wonderful hieroglyphic font in publications such as this.

Picture Credits

The publisher would like to thank the following people, museums, and photographic libraries for permission to reproduce their material. Every care has been taken to trace copyright holders. However, if we have omitted anyone we apologize and will, if informed, make corrections to any future edition.

Abbreviations: BM = © The Trustees of the British Museum. All rights reserved. t = top; b = bottom.

Page 1 BM (EA64661); **7** BM (EA24); **16** Carola Schneider/Gabana Studios Germany; **18t** BM (EA9901,1); **18b** BM (EA10183); **19** BM (EA10508); **20** BM (EA71005/3); **24** BM (EA35597); **58** Ancient Egypt Picture Library/Robert Partridge; **60** BM (EA55586); **62** BM (EA117); **64** Art Archive/Gianni Dagli Orti; **66** Werner Forman Archive/E. Strouhal; **68** Museo Archeologico, Florence/AKG-images/Rabatti-Domingie; **70** Werner Forman Archive/E. Strouhal; **74** Louvre, Paris/© RMN/Hervé Lewandowski (E15591; E22745; C246); **76** Art Archive/Gianni Dagli Orti; **80** Elvira Kronlob/Gabana Studios Germany; **82** Egyptian Museum, Cairo/Jürgen Liepe, Berlin (JE32018); **84–85** Louvre, Paris/© RMN/Daniel Arnaudet /Gérard Blot (E13983); **88** AKG-images/François Guénet; **91** BM (1857,0811.2); **94** Corbis/Charles & Josette Lenars; **98** Art Archive/Gianni Dagli Orti; **100** © National Museums, Liverpool/World Museum (M13860); **102** BM (EA64661); **104** Aegyptisches Museum, Staatliche Museen zu Berlin/© Bildarchiv Foto Marburg (ÄM16953); **108** Aegyptisches Museum, Staatliche Museen zu Berlin/© 2009 Scala, Florence/BPK, Bildagentur für Kunst, Kultur und Geschichte, Berlin/Photo Sandra Steiss (ÄM7265); **110** BM (EA480); **114 all** BM (EA9901/3); **118** Joachim Willeitner, Groebenzell